I AM MAGI

Seeker of Truth

Rhonda Quillin

xulon PRESS

INTRODUCTION

My Ancient World

It is the 15th year of the rule of Roman Emperor Tiberius; Pontius Pilate is governor of Judea, and Herod is still the puppet ruler of Galilee.

I am Balthazar, Royal Magi, King of Arabia. The heavens have summoned two other magi and me to the birth of a divine king to offer our allegiance.

We go because we believe the ancient prophecies that foretell Him. We know He is the mighty divine king who will overthrow governments, save his people and establish his own kingdom that will endure forever.

I am leaving my kingdom and my family seeking this royal newborn, following his herald. The journey is dangerous. The desert is unforgiving; caravans can get lost, be attacked by thieves or be destroyed by massive sandstorms and never seen again.

Caravan Travelers

The Households

Balthazar, Royal Mage, King of Arabia
Caspar, Royal Mage, Maharaja of India and its lands
Melchior, Royal Mage, King of Egypt

Balthazar's Household

His Royal Highness, Royal Mage, *King Balthazar* of Arabia
Her Royal Highness, *Queen Deborah* – Balthazar's wife, mother of the royal heir
His Royal Highness, *Prince Jabael* – royal heir

Sebastian – royal scholar and advisor, Balthazar's close friend
Illya – Balthazar's personal servant and confidant

Shadrach – Commander, King's Guards and personal security
Madai – Commander, Infantry and caravan security

Japheth – navigator
Keenai –overseer of the food supplies
Eleazar – scribe, keeper of the celestial maps and ancient scrolls

Merriam – Deborah's lady's maid
Priscilla – Royal seamstress, precious fabrics and silk expert

Shepherds – usually very young or very old, often stayed with the animals

"Ask, and it will be given to you; seek, and you will find; knock, and it will be opened to you."

Matthew 7:7

Week 1

Balthazar

I AM MAGI, a wealthy king, an educated priest, and privileged beyond any imagination. I am the undisputed ruler of a beautiful, prosperous country that is known for its dependable caravan trade routes that allow it to be the marketplace for the world. I study all things such as religion, medicine, and physics. Two others and I study the heavens and the movements of the planets and stars, what you might call astrology, because we believe divine messages are revealed through them.

My name is Balthazar, King of Arabia and I am a seeker of truth. As the first born of the King and Queen of Arabia, I was welcomed into the world at my birth with royalty and magi paying homage to me.

I had advisors and teachers from a young age and I was given the most advanced education available. I became intrigued with learning and was a prodigy. Then, I saw the advantages of being a soldier and since a sovereign warrior prince is not unusual, my parents changed my academic and political studies to include intense military training.

I started at one of the lowest levels in the Army; well, as low a level as the crown prince accompanied by his servants and advisors could be, and I quickly learned even the prince can be pummeled and cut up when fighting. So I started leaving my servants and advisors behind and began training as hard as any other soldier. That was the beginning of some of the best times of my life; I liked fighting with good soldiers for a good cause. I became a skilled warrior and had the loyalty of excellent troops.

One day my advisor Sebastian and I were debating the next steps in my learning. "Your majesty, you have accomplished so much in your education but you must move on. You are a strong and intelligent soldier but you have so much more to learn before your time comes to ascend the throne."

"Sebastian, I don't want to leave the military. I already know how to be king; I should! I have lived in the royal palace with my parents since I was born and have never been away except when I stay in the barracks. I have years and years of all sorts of education and I am finished with that now. I like it here; my friends are here; and you know, we have a good time. I think I will be happy when I reign as a warrior king."

"Sire, you have to know you are mistaken. There is so much more that you must know in order for you to become a king like your father."

I was frustrated and raised my voice, "You have never wanted me to be a soldier, have you Sebastian? You want me to return to the palace, to a dry dusty classroom and listen to years of lectures! I have listened to lectures, now I want to live!"

"Majesty, I only want to advise you to the best of my ability."

"Then say it! You don't want me to be a soldier, you think I could get hurt, possibly die and then where would you be without a student?"

Immediately I knew I had gone too far. I didn't believe I had just questioned my closest advisor and confidant's loyalty to me in such a rude way. I stood up and at the same time Sebastian rose.

I held out a hand toward him, "I'm sorry Sebastian."

He quickly interrupted, "Your majesty, no; it is I who must apologize. I have been too familiar and have overstepped my position."

I rose to extend my arm over his shoulder but he rose following me but he then stepped back to bow deeply in a way that he never did when we were in private.

"Please excuse me, your majesty. I must check on your appointment book, I believe I have left it in another satchel back at the palace. As always, I only want what is best for you and your family so I beg your leave."

"Of course, I know that. Sebastian." He bowed again as he left the room and was gone.

I sat down heavily and sighed. He was right about one thing; I did have a lot to learn before I could ever reign as well as my father. My father may disagree with someone but he would never insult anyone because of their differences and especially one of his most trusted advisors who happened to be a friend, also.

I was alone in the barracks and heard a horse gallop into the compound, and a shout rang out followed by yelling.

I got up as the door opened and the lieutenant entered the room, looking shaky.

"What is it? What has happened? I demanded."

"My lord, it is Capt Shadrach. His horse threw him and he is badly injured. His foot was caught and his leg is broken. The bones broke through the skin and there is blood everywhere, he asks that we don't move him. He is still out in the further training field, I have sent for the doctor but it will be a while because he is in the village."

I had nodded to my aide as I was listening and said to the lieutenant, "It will take forever for him to get out there. Let's go."

Shadrach and I often are a team when we are training. We are friends, he is a furious warrior and someone I trust to have my back. We rode out to the training field as fast as possible. The soldiers in that company were still there and had put up a tent over where Shadrach lay to keep the sun off of him. He was still on the ground and I could see a great pool of blood beneath him. No one dared to move him.

I slid off of my horse before it came to a stop and was walking toward him as I looked over to my aide, "Make sure the physician is on his way. In fact, go and bring him here now. I don't care where he is or what he is doing."

"Yes, majesty; he is in town with the resupply unit. We have sent soldiers for him but I will make sure I get him here."

I reached the tent and kneeled down in the dirt beside Shadrach. Someone immediately brought me a camp chair. I tried to fake a big smile and said in what I hoped was a mocking tone, "Amateur. Just like an amateur. You still need training wheels on your horse!"

As I guessed, he looked up and tried to smirk, "Your majesty, full of compliments, as always." He ended his sentence with a groan, unable to hide the pain any longer. He continued, "Don't let them move me into town! This leg is a mess and I don't want to lose it. I can't lose it. That doctor, he can come here but he has to hurry. This is bad." He grimaced again through clinched teeth and swallowed another groan. His face was bathed in sweat and his skin was pale and clammy.

He had a light blanket over him and he began to shake. One of the men gave him a sip of wine that barely made it to his mouth because his shaking was so bad.

I looked down at his leg and took a deep breath when I saw something that looked like raw steak with two large bones sticking out of the middle of it in the place that I knew his foot should be. The amount of blood covering the ground, soaking everything let me know he had to be very weak. I shifted in the chair and put my hand on his arm, "The medic has tried to stop the bleeding and it hasn't worked; you know that I won't let you die here. A tourniquet will stop it, you know.

"NO! I said no!" he screamed.

He lowered his voice and looked at me in the eyes, "Majesty, Balthazar, we are friends and soldiers. I will lose my foot, it will rot if we tie it off now; please. . .I asked for a little while longer.

"My friend, I will do whatever you want. I don't want to lose you though; but, I know the physician will be here soon. Hold on."

"Your majesty, please allow me to help Capt Shadrach." I looked up to see Sebastian. He had obviously heard about the injury as he was leaving camp and turned back.

"Sebastian! I'm glad you're here."

"Thank you, your majesty." As he was talking, Sebastian made a short bow and quickly moved to Shadrach's other side and was looking intently at his face. He had a small fabric satchel with him that he placed carefully at his side and then opened with one hand as he glanced down at the injured leg. The mangled limb and blood didn't seem to bother him and he didn't mention the foot at all. He looked calm, as if he did this everyday. Several of the men who had been standing around slowly backed away and left, so there were just a couple of onlookers still there.

"Captain, I am here to ease your pain."

Shadrach's eyes were looking glassy and he struggled hard to summon energy in order to croak a response. "Sebastian, I am afraid I made a mess of my leg. It hurts—"

Sebastian leaned close to Shadrach and seemed to brush some dirt from the side of his face as he spoke quietly to him. Then he actually seemed to sniff the remains of the dirt on his hand that he had just brushed off. He paused, then turned quickly to fill a small bowl with liquid from his satchel and then dusted the rim with a crushed leaf. "I have something for you to drink and you will feel sleepy but you won't fall asleep; I'm sorry but I need you to listen to me. First in order to conserve your strength, I don't want you to speak anymore, just blink your eyes once for yes and twice for no."

Sebastian again offered the bowl to his lips, urging him to drink it all. As Shadrach took a deep breath after finishing the drink, Sebastian crushed more of the leaf right under his nose. He dried and returned the bowl to his satchel and when he straightened, he continued. "I need to deal with the bleeding now. Can you hear me?

Shadrach's breathing had become slower and deeper. He blinked once.

His voice had become lower and comforting. "Good. Now listen, I am not going to hurt you. You can trust me. I want you to help by imagining. Listen Shadrach, this is important. Imagine you are sleeping out in the desert and your feet are cold because your blanket is short. Now, you are asleep but you know your feet are cold; in fact, very cold. If you were awake, you would be uncomfortable but you know you are still asleep so you are fine for now.

Sebastian had been systematically arranging other things from his satchel as he talked; now he paused and turned fully to Shadrach's mangled leg. "Good, you are doing fine. He paused a beat and continued, "Now, it is even later and you wake up to find that your feet are so cold that you can't feel them."

Here, I'll put a something on your feet so they will warm up and you can go back to sleep since you don't need to wake up for hours." After saying that, he stopped and looked measuringly at Shadrach's face, then pulled strongly on his ankle. He quickly followed that with picking up something that looked like shears that were laid out close by and opened the strings of the skin on his lower leg that were still in place. There was a rush of dirty fluid and then Sebastian cleaned the area and wrapped and padded it with sheepskin.

Shadrach's eyes had been open, just barely, and he was breathing deep and easy and he didn't seem to notice what Sebastian was doing.

He was awake, but not really and when Sebastian mentioned he could go to sleep, his eyes immediately closed. He was sound asleep! I shook my head because I was getting sleepy and had to stop myself from stomping my feet to warm them. They felt cold! I looked closely at what Sebastian was doing. He finished examining the injured foot and then started cleaning his instruments carefully. The bleeding had stopped!

"Sebastian, how did you do that and what did you do?"

"Majesty, I gave him some suggestions so he would do what he really wanted to do anyway. He wanted the pain to stop."

"But you stopped his bleeding! And you made him sleep!"

"No, he stopped his own bleeding. And he knows if he sleeps that the pain will disappear. Tell me, when you are cold doesn't your skin get pale and generally lose feeling?"

"Yes. But his foot is almost torn off!"

"Balthazar, truths remain. What is true when things are good and you are healthy, is true when bad things happen and you are injured. Cold constricts and a lot of cold constricts even more. So it makes sense to add some cold or the suggestion of cold to a wound and then believe your body will try to stop or slow the blood circulation.

"Capt Shadrach, your feet are warmer now and you are sleeping comfortably, aren't you?

He opened his eyes to blink once then closed them immediately.

I stood up to look closely at his leg, "Is it still broken?"

"Yes your majesty. Some people can actually set their own broken bones, but this isn't the place nor does he have the time to learn to do that now."

I had always known Sebastian was gifted in healing and that he knew much more about people and the power of their minds than anyone else. "But what did you do? Really."

He was closing his satchel and turned to me to speak, "Your majesty, I used the power of his mind to help him. Knowledge, intellect and truth are powerful forces. When we know how to use them, we can accomplish amazing things."

So you used Shadrach's mind to stop his bleeding and control his pain?

"Simply put, yes."

"And you want me to continue my studies so my knowledge and intellect will be powerful forces like this to guide my kingdom?"

"Your majesty, yes."

Week 2

The Royal Herald

After years of studying with Sebastian and other scholars I knew that my path in life would be in pursuit of truth and knowledge. I studied the heavens and knew prophecies were revealed through their alignments and I found that I could read the stars to see truth and often, the future.

Sebastian was still my teacher and advisor and he had been the one standing to my left when I had been offered the title of Royal Magi. He had watched while the emblem of magi had been added to my golden crown and had been placed below my birth tattoo on my forearm.

I and two other magi, Caspar and Melchior, have since formed a friendship through the study of ancient scrolls; we also search the heavens, and debate the latest ideas and theories with the most intelligent scholars of our time. We know about the prophecy of a divine king and we believe he will be born soon. We have spent hours searching for information by locating ancient old manuscripts, visiting temple libraries, and reading star charts.

We learned that this king will be like no other; he will rise up and shift the power here on earth from Rome to establish his own kingdom. His kingdom will be great beyond any other; because he will rule in peace and there will be no more disease or hunger; he will rule as King of kings.

Where the child will be born is still a mystery to us; we personally know all of the other royal families and we have heard no announcements. So as royalty, it is very important that we align ourselves and our lands with this king who is destined to rule everyone. As magi, it is very important to continue to seek and to learn truth. So we wait and watch. For what? His herald.

~~~~~~~~~~~~~~~~~~~~

It happened last night! As usual, we had gathered in our old tower to watch and study the heavens for His sign. I had brought several more scrolls that detailed the prophet Isaiah's writings and wanted to argue some points with Caspar.

Caspar, Royal Mage, Maharaja of India and its lands represents a huge and ancient household. He is my friend and confidant, he was born exactly two years before me and our families are bound by centuries of marriages and trade treaties. The exact size and reach of his kingdom has varied so much throughout history that it is commonly thought that he may be somewhat related to the royal newborn.

After all, how many royal families are there?

Even though he is descended from one of the strongest ruling houses, Caspar has found that truth and knowledge is key to being a good ruler. He travels the world in order to learn from the greatest scholars and this quest has humbled him. His gifts include his powerful intellect and vision that allow him to prophecy with complete accuracy.

So Caspar and I have both set up star charts showing where we believe the stars will align when the time had come for the royal birth. Both were now exactly mirroring the heavens as we strained to peer into the gathering darkness above.

The others were already there when I climbed the steps, accompanied by Sebastian and my other servants.

Caspar leaned over the balcony when he saw me arrive, "The sky is filled with stars tonight! They seem to have all gathered together so they look like one mass; I'm not sure where to train the telescope."

"It is so clear tonight, they look close enough to touch," I agreed.

Melchior sighed and was already at his desk, inking another chart. "But don't you feel it? There is something different happening. It's as if excitement is building in the heavens and everything is waiting."

We all agreed, but would these stars and planets be content to wait centuries? Or is the time now?

My servant was busy pulling scrolls from a bag and handing them to Sebastian. I remembered an old star chart that described where constellations were positioned in the ancient times so as Caspar was setting up his instruments; I dug through the parchments lying on a nearby table and turned to Melchior.

"See, I found the text that describes how your family named the constellation after your father. . ." I had placed a weight at an edge of the scroll and Melchior picked up another to place at the other end. However, it rolled out of his reach and dropped off the table, so I bent down to pick it up. Straightening, we both turned at Caspar's gasp; he had abandoned his telescope and was gazing out at the western night sky with his mouth open.

I didn't see anything different at first but I quickly saw that the darkness seemed to be trembling!

Then we all saw it, some kind of new star patterns, unlike any other we had ever seen. The stars that blanket the evening sky over the desert, the ones that are spread out as far as the eye could see, now these very same stars were growing fast!

As they grew, they began to flash brilliantly and they started to move toward each other and swirl around and around, as more stars joined them from all over the sky. The light grew as thousands stars joined in swirling around and around something in the middle. We could hear "whoosh" each time one of them came close in their flight. We all staggered back against the wall directly across from the open balcony, as stars blazed across the sky to join the others.

I don't know how long that lasted, surely not more than a few minutes. Soon the stars that were swirling toward each other joined as they all melded into one gigantic star-shape that eventually consumed an entire section of the western sky with blazing beauty.

This light didn't look like another planet or star. It looked like it was alive; it was stretching and against all usual laws of nature, moved north across the western sky where it stopped and stood completely still. In a minute it rotated and a huge axis appeared through the dark and large beams of light burst out joining heaven and earth! The star's brilliance continued to grow as its light reflected off of other heavenly bodies; occasionally its massive tail would fan out and dust the sky with thousands of brilliant newborn stars. The movement looked joyous and unearthly.

Melchior had slid down the wall into a chair, watching with amazement. "He beckons. It is His herald," he said without moving his eyes from the celebration in the sky. He then stood and leaned over the balcony, looking up without a telescope. He gazed in wonder, laughing at times at the mystery of the antics of these stars.

Finally he raised both of his arms declaring to all who could hear his great voice, "His messengers are the heavens and they have been given the privilege of proclaiming his pending birth. Behold, the herald is here, soon the divine Son of the God of Heaven will be born."

Melchior was always the cautious one, he is the elder royal mage who had powers of healing and mind control far above anyone else's abilities, even those of Sebastian. So when he declared this was indeed the message we had been waiting for, we got busy.

I came to my senses and quickly calibrated the direction of the lights. We would be following this amazing light and if we had to travel before night at any time in the caravan, we didn't want to have to guess where it had been. Then I just stared.

21

"What kind of king is able to direct the heavens? What can I offer him in friendship?"

Caspar was mesmerized watching the ecstatic heavens and still hadn't moved but he called over, "Balthazar, is your household is ready? We leave tomorrow."

"Of course I am ready. You just remember to show up at the crossroads or you will be left behind to watch me in one of your visions!"

Caspar's servant was quickly packed his scrolls and ink, "Ha! No chance of that."

Melchior gazed quietly for a few moments longer at the heavens. By now the newborn stars were randomly dancing across the sky. Some seemed to finally cartwheel right into the center of the huge beacon, adding to its brightness. The beacon itself had settled into a star-shape that moved with an energy unknown in the heavens. It occasionally seemed to flash and move as if it were alive and singing.

I grabbed my small star gazer and charts and bounded down the stairs from the balcony two at a time, chased by Sebastian at a distance.

Once on the ground, despite my privilege and royal status, I ran; literally ran to my waiting servants, scaring them half to death, shouting "We go! Hurry, hurry, we must be back at the palace—every last thing should be packed as soon as possible. Where is—"

"Here I am, my lord. All is ready. The entire household is ready: food, water and animals, tents and furniture, clothing and necessary supplies. And your jewels and gift will be close, of course."

Illya, my body and household servant was talking to my back because I had turned toward Melchior and Caspar, and called out. "Ok, at the caravan crossroads before dusk. I will be ready, will you?"

Melchior was still looking up at the blazing star, "Go home Balthazar, say goodbye to your family. They will miss you during your journey, and you will miss them. So, take some time. We will make sure we have all of the tablets and scrolls that we will need for our studies."

~~~~~~~~~~~~~~~~~~~

Back at the palace I am still scrambling in my undignified haste as my servants stop and stare open-mouthed. Suddenly, I stop dead in my tracks; although it is very late, I have to go see my wife. She has to know my journey starts tomorrow.

My heart expands with love as I think of her—what a good wife and life-partner she is. She is just right for me; we have been blessed with strong, obedient sons. I am thankful for them and I love them. Then, years after the sons came a daughter. I always thought it would be good politics to have a daughter to help run the household and to create alliances, but she is so much more. She is the goodness and tenderness that I have always hoped to be, she says good morning to me and the sun shines; she says she loves me and my heart sings. My glances linger on her when I don't think she is looking.

To our sorrow, however, she is fragile—she has an illness and she is failing. Our beautiful daughter! We have found no cure despite all of my searching, and I am afraid of what may happen.

So, even though this is a joyous journey to be summoned to worship a newborn king, it is difficult to leave my family. My wife and sons will understand and my daughter will, also, but I hate to leave when I know I may never see the little precious one again.

I straighten up when I realize once again that no matter what, I must go because I have been summoned. There can be no excuse given.

"Illya, we meet with Melchior and Caspar tomorrow evening while it is still light at the crossroad foothills west of here. Since the caravan is so large, make sure my household master, foreman, and troops meet with us every night to report. And as always, you personally will be in charge of my books, telescope and maps."

I continue to babble in excitement as I stand still so my servant can remove my robes to exchange for indoor garments. He removes my outer robe that protects me from the sand that is always present, and from the cold here in the desert at night. It is dark and heavy, and as I raise an arm so it can be whisked away, I realize I can hear more and more movement around the palace as supplies are being prepared and the caravan is loaded. I have to remember to bring that old robe that was my father's, it is heavy and will be a comfort.

Illya goes to another servant who has just come to the hall and listens, then nods. "Majesty, your Lady is awake and has asked for you. Will you let me help you refresh yourself and change your inner robe before you attend her?"

"Deborah is awake? Yes, please tell her I am on my way."

Of course Deborah would know something amazing has happened. She has powers of her own and always knows when great moments occur. Thinking back to when I met her, I shake my head. I wasn't very interested when the inevitable day arrived that I was summoned by my parents to meet my fiancé. I knew that my path in life as a mage would be in pursuit of truth and knowledge, so I thought I wouldn't be affected personally by a betrothal! This was the life of royalty, marriage was a political alliance and it would have nothing to do with me personally.

I wasn't very interested in which princess was chosen, so I was astounded to find that I fell in love! The woman that I met was nothing like the dry politically aligned princess that I had come to expect.

First, the lady was beautiful and smart. But did I say she was beautiful? The first time I saw her, she was presented along with her parents in my mother's reception rooms. I was prepared to act correctly as was required but more importantly to listen carefully to the terms of the proposed alliance. So when the lady followed her parents into the room, I immediately saw her beauty and natural intelligence in her lovely form and face.

I'm afraid I was so busy staring at her that I stumbled slightly when I rose to greet her and her parents. I was relieved at first that I was able to grab Sebastian's arm in order to steady myself. It was too bad that even then I was a lot bigger than he was so that my weight on his arm caused us we both to stumble into one my mother's favorite vases. As others gasped and hurried over to help us both up, the lady burst out in giggles that she tried in vain to cover with her hand while her parents stood staring in horror at me. So I'm afraid that my first impression wasn't very grand.

When we were given an opportunity to speak to each other, she told me that her given name was Deborah. I finally came up with my own name after a few tries; my problem was that it was difficult to look at her and think clearly at the same time.

So instead of me intelligently mentioning superficial matters, she immediately began to ask me questions as if she were interviewing me; just as though she would be the one to decide whether to accept my betrothal or not! I was thankful that I was able to tear my gaze away from her eyes in order to try to respond to at least some of her questions and then offer a comment or two. But I don't remember a thing that we said.

To my amazement, she became my bride! So instead of only a political alliance, ours is also a love match.

~~~~~~~~~~~~~~~~~~~~~

My servant patiently began again, "Majesty, please let me assist you into a bath and a change of gowns before you—"

"Here, I'll help," Illya had appeared at the servant's side to order to get Balthazar redressed in the fashion he should be in order to see his wife. The servant quickly departed and Illya turned back to look at Balthazar, standing completely naked as he was picking through pile after pile of clothing that had been set out to be packed.

"Your highness, would you stop! Please let me dress you so you can visit your lady. Otherwise she will blame me that you didn't come to her or she will berate me for not caring for you correctly and what will I be able to say, my lord?"

"My mind is flying back and forth among so many bits of information that I can hardly stand still. Illya, it has finally happened! And I know this is my destiny, I will never be the same. Where are my overcoats? Have they been packed?"

Illya has been my personal servant and confidant since I was a boy; we were given the exact same education, were taught how to ride horses and camels by the same trainers and entered the military together. His job now is to be closer than any servant or advisor can be, he is always at my side and never far away.

He is my age and stature, cultured, royally-educated and wealthy. He also has the powerful position of sovereign confidant. There is nothing that he doesn't know about me and vice versa. We both know either of us would die before we would give up these secrets. We have lived in the same household since early childhood and we know we will not be separated for any reason, ever. So he knows how to get my attention.

"Majesty, yes; I have your coats ready, they are in the first basket of outer garments. However; right now, please understand that I must ready you immediately to see your wife. Otherwise, birth of a divine king or not, I am much more afraid of what your lady will do to me."

I stopped, "Right. Illya, you are making a lot of sense. OK. Where is my robe?" He had been standing right in front of me with my gown held in his hands.

As I stood still long enough for Illya to drape the robe and wave for another servant to adjust slippers on my feet, I mused. "I must carefully keep notes of everything that happens on this wondrous journey. This journal will be my story to future generations and to the entire world."

Week 3

Travelers Attacked

The magi and their households, the servants, staffs, and supplies, they would need for the journey met at the head of the caravan route at the edge of town the next day as dusk was falling. Everyone was excited because it was well know that they would be a part of greeting the newborn divine king. All had said goodbye to their families and were now making the final checks to their security, provisions, and plans.

Everything was in order; the caravan chief approached the magi and their staffs. He paused because he had never been so close to royalty before. He had seen mighty King Balthazar's palace and had heard of magi but never thought they would be at his caravan dock. He bowed to all and finally looked to Illya and was motioned for him to continue. "Your majesties, all is ready. Do I have your leave to start?"

The massive caravan that included three royal households moved out into the miles of dark desert.

~~~~~~~~~~~~~~~~~~~~

The caravan slowly gained momentum as the magi continued to map the star and update their charts. Finally, there was mostly quiet as they contemplated their next move.

Hours later Caspar broke the quiet, "It is still dark, but the sun will come up soon. What are your thoughts? Shall we stop during the day, waiting for the star to return to guide us at night? Or navigate by your star map during the day?"

Balthazar raised his face to the nighttime sky, searching for an answer. Seeing only the magnificent star and dark night he replied,

"I don't know, but I believe something unusual will happen with the rising of the sun. I can't find any mention of any of this in the ancient writings, we are living a miracle. But I know this brilliant jewel in the sky is moving, urging us to follow. Let's continue for an hour more, and then decide if we can brave the desert sun if the jewel keeps beckoning."

"Pardon, Your highness, I am still unsure exactly where you mean for us to go; I don't know where you want us to end up," this question came from within the small group of men surrounding the magi as they rode in their caravan through the night.

"Japheth, you are asking for our destination, is that right?" Japheth was a trusted navigator. Even though he was a slightly built man who looked as though he had never been out of the city, he had personally mapped and traveled through the desert for over 50 years.

"Well, your majesty. A thousand pardons, but yes! It's just. . .how can I lead us? The desert is a hostile place and I need to find the quickest and safest path to where we are going. Please tell me more than "follow the star in the western sky". Maps, you see, I have maps but I have to know where to stop for water, which villages to go to replenish our supplies and where to avoid shifting sands."

Madai, the Infantry Commander, appeared alongside them in the darkness, "You donkey," he railed at Japheth, "You mean you haven't mapped our travels? This is a dangerous area for a caravan and there are too many bandits who wait for those like us to ambush, to steal from, to murder, or just to torture for their own entertainment. Get on it! I can't keep us alive if you are personally going to deliver us to thieves!"

"We don't yet know our destination, we aren't following a map. We are following that star," Balthazar said, glancing up toward the sky and not looking at their shocked faces.

"What? I mean, pardon your Highness, but please tell us what is on your mind. This is suicidal. What will happen when the sun rises or the night is cloudy, or there is a sandstorm, or a million other things that can and will happen?"

"Then we will watch and wait." And with that answer, all discussion stopped.

Every sound is magnified in the desert at night, and sounds can travel distances to unfriendly ears; so for safety most caravans try to keep as quiet as possible. Often hours go by with only the sound of animals breathing and leather creaking. It's safer this way.

Caspar, like the other magi, was atop a large camel. In the gloom, he was only slightly visible since he was toward the front of the line and ahead of Balthazar quite a few paces. He stirred and suddenly sat up straight in his saddle and called out "Look!" creating a small panic among the camels.

The inky sky had begun to slowly lighten with the coming day, and Caspar had been trying to measure the star that reached down toward the ground when it started to change before his eyes. The long vertical axis that had frequently flashed and stretched throughout the night while urging them forward had started telescoping in, becoming broader and looking more like a lamp. The tapered horizontal arms moved up to join the topmost part of the star to become a glowing golden beacon, resting and still. Yet it was still supernaturally bright so that it continued to impose itself on the gathering daylight.

The caravan continued its slow monotonous movement throughout the star's transformation, so Balthazar was soon up alongside the others again,

"There it is, our answer. We will rest in the day during the worst of the heat, and the beacon will still shine through the daylight when we want to map it. I can still see it in the sunlight! We will travel only when it guides us, so for now we will rest and be still."

Turning to Japheth he continued, "This is our plan; don't worry. We are guided by the beacon, it moves to show us the direction to travel but how we get there is up to us. Yes, we need your best and latest maps and we will stop as needed for the most current information; we will avoid what we need to avoid, but we will follow the light."

Caravans don't do anything quickly. Scouts are first sent ahead, and also left behind so once the caravan is traveling, a chain of scouts and riders on camels or horses are going out and returning regularly. Communication is essential for everyone's safety. There are caravan routes, which are just worn places across the desert that travelers follow in order to maintain some contact with small villages and other caravans.

Caspar and his household rode at the front of the caravan. Caspar traveled just like the other two magi, with a multitude of attendants and servants. He had flocks also that accompanied him, cooks, consulting scholars, advisors, and body servants. He carried fabrics and jewels in order to have glorious clothing made when it was time to be presented to the royal family and the Divine Newborn. This would be the most significant event of his life and he was a member of one of the oldest royal families known, so he would act and look like the royal person that he was.

Caspar knew that the camel behind him to his right carried a leather satchel that carried a gift that was a prize beyond anything most people had ever seen. His family's royal gift to present to the Newborn was sitting in a jewel-encrusted cask in a satchel. Even though it was a unique and priceless gift, Caspar had an idea that the Newborn's father, whoever He was, was be willing to give even more astonishing gifts to those who came to greet and honor His Son.

Caspar had the gift of prophecy; he often heard and saw angels, people, and things that no one else could see and he often felt as though he belonged in both this world and that other one that he visited in his prophecies and visions. He often was able to see past what was going on in the here and now because of the visions that came to him. Caspar shook his head, "Who is this King? And how will we find Him?"

As the caravan was creaking to a slow stop, those at the end of the line made a typical sweep so the entire caravan line looked like a large crescent. They were preparing to stop for the day, not just a pause or rest and this formation was designed with safety in mind.

In minutes however, shouting and frantic activity erupted near the soldiers at the front of the line that juts out from the passengers and camels; it was obvious someone with news had returned to the camp.

Balthazar looked to his staff for information and Illya appeared at Balthazar's side, walking with him to the men surrounding the rider,

"Your majesty! Our scouts! Something has happened; only one has returned and he is severely wounded."

Since Balthazar had lived the life of a soldier prince, one who fought to expand his family's lands and power, he could recognize the wounds on the man they were putting into a hastily erected tent. He had defensive cuts on his arms and a ragged short sword wound at his stomach. He knew these were the marks of a fight against someone who didn't have a Roman-issued weapon nor did he have the money for a better sword.

"Melchior, we need your help here."

Melchior was already striding toward the tent, and was quickly beside Balthazar, "Of course. What happened? And where are the others?" he asked as he bent to examine the bleeding man.

He started talking to the injured man in a low voice. He didn't pause and sometimes he asked questions, but mostly gave instructions. Sometime he gave odd directions like the man should think of the color blue, a deep blue, very strongly, right now. Then the soldier grew calm and placid and very trusting.

Melchior's voice was soft and low, "Perhaps it's time for the bleeding to stop." It stopped.

Then he reminded the soldier, "It's all right to take slow deep breaths and to then close your eyes to sleep." He did.

This is his way, he diverted the wounded man's mind with simple questions and conversation as he examined and removed the gore of the gaping wounds. He employed his salve, medicines, and bandages; then finished with a subtle glance at the patient and a hypnotic suggestion, "You are feeling much better and really want to rest quietly to heal. The combination of medications, technique and healing suggestions usually worked.

After a while Melchior looked up at Balthazar and nodded his head. Maybe this man would live.

Balthazar turned to Madai as he spoke, "Your majesty, there are no others left alive. This man was able to tell us that there is a large band of thieves over the next hill, maybe just an hour away. They are waiting by the water waiting for caravans and there is a small village nearby, but we can't go there because it is home to these bandits and will be no help. The soldiers had approached the oasis and were asking about buying food nearby when they were attacked."

Madai continued the report "I have dispatched other scouts besides just this group. They should already be in the village and along the caravan route; I'll send word to them to be prepared.

"Joaz, take your men and intercept our soldiers. Let me know what they say. Send a rider back to the palace to secure it in case of an attack there, just in case this is part of something bigger that means harm at home. Double the guards around us and the supply lines and send a group to search for marauders. Be quick now, before they get away. When you catch a straggler, find out everything you can."

Before the next soldiers went out, there was the sound of hooves beating the sand followed by the shouts of attackers. The horizon was filled with sand and the sound was deafening as a veritable army of bandits descended on the stopped caravan. People scattered everywhere, animals bleated and brayed, straining to break away and camels shook to free themselves from leads and escape the uproar.

"Take cover!"

"Soldiers, collapse the caravan length and form the defense. Columns intact? You others, keep hold of those camels and Joaz I need your report." Shadrach had been in service to Balthazar's family for years. Soon after Balthazar left military service he was offered the position in the King's Guards, an elite fighting unit. It was at times like this that it was good to know that his lord Balthazar had been a soldier long before he took up his crown and because of that he knew what to do.

Balthazar immediately set up a command tent, secured the caravan household and sent word that he required immediate and up-to-date reports.

The attack was unexpected and, of course, an attack on a caravan always goes well for the bandits at first. They have the freedom of surprise, mobility and planning. The trick was to turn it around before too much damage was done. The sounds of fighting continued; the panicked animals fought as hard as the attackers and the screams of the wounded were heard as spears found their way around shields.

The caravan was made up of the magi's household servants and attendants. They also had herds of sheep and cattle, supplies, and personal items with them. The reason this one was so big was that it contained three full caravan households. It wasn't a trading enterprise so there wasn't any reason to attack it except to plunder and murder. If they lost the fight, they and their households would just never been seen again. The magi wouldn't be ransomed; the thieves knew they would be killed immediately if they dared to hostage a king.

Joaz slid off of his horse and reported to Shadrach, "Sir, we are being attacked from the south only and they are well armed. I don't know who they are: bandits or a remnant of an army. I'm still gathering information, but we have formed our defensive position."

Shadrach knew first reports are always wrong, "Keep firing from our defensive posture; but don't let them get away, either. You understand; I want to know who they are. As soon as possible, on my word, we go forward. And as soon as you get the next report, come back to me."

The caravan seemed to continue to sit in a defensive position with little response and it started to lull the attackers into coming closer. Shadrach was waiting for one or two of the riders to attempt into break into the fortified area of the caravan and then they would have them.

Instead, after a few half-hearted attempts to breach the caravan perimeter, the attackers just rode off. Shadrach watched them carefully as they left and followed the path over the next hill. He desperately wanted to be in charge of the riders sent to chase down the attackers, but he also knew that was not a good plan. The bandits could be planning to circle back to the caravan to attack when the defenses were down or the pursuers could be led back to an entire army and butchered.

The shrieks from the wounded in the caravan had started to die down as the next report came in, "The attackers inflicted no other casualties, they tried to stampede our animals, but they didn't succeed there either. We've had some injuries and we are treating them now. One of the shepherd boys was wounded. He took a club in the face and he will lose at least one eye, and he will probably be blind in the remaining one."

Another rider came in with important news. Shadrach strode over to Balthazar's tent, "Your majesties, I have had word from the scouts. It seems that we are following a route that leads us through a war zone. We found a wounded man, he claims he isn't a thief but is part of the struggle of one fiefdom against another. One group has claims to the land due south, the other says it was stolen from them and they mean to reclaim it.

Sire, the answer here is simple; we can just change our course; even though it may mean traveling in another direction for days. We don't want to be involved in this and in this manner we can avoid it altogether."

To Shadrach's surprise, Melchior shook his head and the other magi agreed, "No. This isn't that simple, we are being guided by the star. It's not a matter that we can alter our course and reach the end of our journey from a different route.

He continued, "Balthazar, you know the maps and paths around the caravan routes better than anyone. We are aware that we don't know our final destination. Is there any way to avoid this area but still follow as the beacon directs?"

Balthazar was looking at the maps again with Japheth. He turned, "I have every map in our possession in front of me now, Melchior, if there was another possible route, Japheth would know it and he says there is none."

Caspar had been deep in thought with his fingers steepled in front of his face. "My friends, what does this tell us? It is saying with divine authority that we will go through this trouble and live to worship the newborn. It doesn't say this will be easy, or there will be no losses and there won't be frightening times—it says trust and believe. We will be guided."

"Caspar, you are right. We will continue to follow where the star leads."

"Shadrach, secure the caravan and continue your work; we will follow this path even though it seems to be a dangerous one for now," said Balthazar.

"Yes, your majesty; I just hope we are not following a path to our death."

Week 4

Letter Home

𝒮𝕣

"I have another bag for the courier returning to the palace tonight, Illya, make sure it is taken and given to my wife," Balthazar finished rolling up a scroll destined for his family. He knew that any royal missive from the caravan would be shared with many at the palace, so he didn't write the note himself. He dictated it to his scribes, who were fluent in the traditional writing forms of the royal houses, but it still just didn't share what he truly wanted to say. There were no loving phrases or any place for intimate details so he hoped that when Deborah was reading the dry words and the endless royal posturing, that she somehow would know what he really wanted to tell her.

With the completion of his letter, Balthazar fell into a deep sleep and dreamed. He dreamed of the Newborn and a kingdom without end; he could see that the infant was of the royal line of King David, a son of Abraham, and that he would be a royal priest to his people forever.

He awoke with renewed energy—they were following the herald of a royal priest, a king and his new kingdom; so that must mean the Newborn was magi! Surely if they would arrive to worship the Newborn and be presented to the royal household, they would be offered power, alliances, and maybe the knowledge and services of magi skilled in medicine in order to heal his daughter. When recognized as a friend by the King of kings, only good things would happen for his kingdom, family and himself.

Week 5

Fourteen

raveling through the cool darkness of night, the magi were talking about the newborn and wondering why they didn't know which royal family He represented. They were each covered in their heavy wraps and their voices carried easily in the desert as they followed their great star beckoning in the west.

Caspar turned to the others as he continued the conversation, "Think! Just how many royal families are there? There aren't that many so aren't you mystified that the Newborn's arrival is such a secret? There should be great rejoicing but yet there is nothing but silence from these palaces."

"I believe this mystery means that our Newborn King is destined to lead the great rebellion to rescue His people, establish His kingdom, and change the world as we know it. We are rushing to the presentation of the long-awaited King who will free His people from the lash of the Romans. Perhaps that is what is written in the stars, a mighty king will be born, a warrior prince that his family will protect until his time comes, and then war, again!" suggested Balthazar.

Melchior, always the peacekeeper, countered, "My friends, don't you think that He is somehow something much more? I truly hope so! A royal messiah sent from heaven to find and save the Jews is so much more than just another revolutionary."

Illya approached them, "My Lord Balthazar, Priscilla is here, about your jewels and garments for when you are presented to the newborn king and his household."

The men stopped their conversation, and looked over at Balthazar. Even in the gloom, he studiously avoided their glances, "I'm sure they are fine. I don't need a report now," as he glanced away.

"My lord", Illya's voice turned to a whisper, "she is already here and she won't take no for an answer. Please! Please just see her. Then maybe she will just go away."

Balthazar sighed; this was becoming tedious, "All right, bring her to me."

The seamstress who accompanied Illya was beautiful and she carried herself with pride. Most wives would have worried about a beautiful servant girl accompanying her husband on a long journey but Deborah was different. She could judge how true a person's heart was and she had handpicked Priscilla to accompany the caravan because of her great skill in managing fabrics. Her work was always beautiful, no matter what it was and who it arrayed. Deborah was sure that she was the one to accompany the caravan and to create the royal garments.

Not only was Priscilla beautiful but she was intelligent and loyal, and she understood the importance of her work. She was aware that royalty often had to fight to keep their countries intact and a ruler had to be stronger than the others who attempted to take their lands. It could mean disaster for Balthazar if he ever showed a hint of weakness or didn't look like a strong and confident monarch. Even during this time of celebrating a royal birth, danger would lurk so he must always look every inch like the powerful ruler that he was, especially when he was presented to the family to honor their newborn.

Priscilla knew how to convey power and prestige through the array of robes and accessories she intended to create for Balthazar. It was a valuable part of keeping the entire household safe to exhibit his wealth and the power he commanded. She would not belittle her position and she would not allow a mere body servant as Illya to even think he could stop her from her duty to Lord Balthazar's house.

"Your highness, I am reporting that all of the jewels and fabrics that I carry for your garments are safe. I have kept everything from harm so nothing was damaged in the least and remains in readiness. Please allow Illya to notify me when to plan your fitting, so we may decide which of your jewels you should wear. If would be terrible if we allowed another court's attire to outshine your garments so that you don't appear as you should.

As Balthazar nodded his head, Priscilla bowed slightly and turned back after she glared at Illya who blocked her way until she was dismissed to leave, she continued "You may be assured that no matter how high-born another king is, no matter how lofty is another court, your garments and jewels will reflect your august status. And, I will ensure that the jewels and fabrics you wear will only augment your appearance, to your glory."

"Thank you, that is all," Balthazar said.

Watching her take her leave and stalk back through the shadowy caravan, Caspar shook his head. "I didn't know why Deborah insisted on this seamstress accompanying us; she is always rude and argumentative. Ha! But now I find myself wishing for someone who would bow and say they will ensure my garments reflect my status."

Balthazar sighed, "I must speak to Deborah about her, however. Maybe she can do something about her seamstress who seems to delight in frightening Illya!

The magi were still laughing as Illya sniffed and quietly left their side after a few moments. They returned to the previous subject and Caspar offered, "Once our couriers have located the Newborn's royal household, we can begin to inquire to be presented and then have our garments made for our presentation. I believe they will need to be unlike anything we have ever had, and we must, of course, bring our presents that should outshine the jewels we are wearing.

And Melchior, don't think I haven't seen the ostrich-egg opal that you are fond of wearing. Beware, it may catch the eye of someone in the newborn's household and if it was admired, how could you say no?"

Even in the dark they could see Melchior turn pale, "Do you think—"

The other two laughed and Caspar continued, "Melchior you are incredible! I don't honestly think you should be afraid that the Newborn will swipe your jewelry, but I do love to see you worry!"

"It's not that I thought it would be stolen. Well, maybe. Just for a minute. Perhaps it would be safer if I didn't wear that particular stone, it is so beautiful. I have many others."

It was well known that Melchior's lands were rich in fantastic jewels and that he enjoyed wearing them. As King of Persia, he had the right to all of his country's wealth, but sometimes they thought he liked jewels a little too much.

Melchior's soft dreamlike voice replied, "I cannot even begin to imagine what the Newborn's court will be like. He will be the descendent of so many kings and to be king of all. Such majesty, such knowledge of all things! I long to be able to study and discuss ideas with other magi. We will find truth. I know it. I long to understand the wonders of our world and universe; I may need to stay a long time in the palace of our mighty newborn King and I will pay whatever tribute is required to learn these mysteries.

It was quiet for a while.

Caspar looked over, "But Melchior, what is it? Why do you look like that? This is a joyous occasion and suddenly you look so unhappy."

"My friend, I am not unhappy. Why do I look like this? I have just had a revelation, look instead at the skies; look at the star. Read the ancient scrolls. I have come to believe that the newborn King is not who we have ignorantly thought He is. Perhaps we have not heard any news from the royal households that we communicate with because He is not of any of the existing households.

Balthazar replied, "He must. We know it has been written that He will be the 14th generation descendent in a royal house."

Melchior answered, "Yes, but our question continues to be of which house? If we count generations, finding significant signs in each 14th generation, the only possible answer is the Jewish household of King David, royal son of father Abraham."

"There is no Jewish royal household," argued Caspar, "not one that isn't run by the Romans. This is well known."

Then we were all talking at once, mystified that Melchior was well on his way to unraveling many of the questions.

"Look! The 14th generation is significant only within one specific family. Look, we know the generations between the warrior, King David to now, but go back into the mist of time. Generations from Abraham to King David: 14! Generations from King Solomon until Jews were defeated and taken to Babylon: 14! And finally, 14 appears again when you count the generations from their captivity until now."

Melchior continued, "So we are talking about the Jewish royal line, it is the only answer that makes sense. So we ask why the Jews instead of any other people? The answer has to be in what the prophets of their God say, that the Jews are His special people. We know that they have been proclaiming a coming king for centuries and we know that because we study their prophecies! And we study their prophecies because they all come true! Because every single one of the prophecies have come to pass, every single one has been fulfilled and now the prophecy of a warrior king that will establish his own kingdom is going to happen!

However, as I see it, the facts are these: First, there is no longer an established Jewish royal household since they don't govern themselves; and their so-called rulers are Roman puppets. Second, the Newborn will not be Roman! We have seen what they do to those who proclaim themselves king instead of bow to their emperor.

So, we need to make a choice here and now. Will we obey the commands of the Lord of the universe and continue to follow the herald announcing His son's birth, to honor Him? If so, we should be aware that we are riding into an uneven contest here because Rome will not ignore the claims of this royal Newborn for long. Or do we contemplate another manner of welcoming the King? One much safer for us and our families since we all have much to lose?"

The conversation had quickly become as dark and gloomy as the night around them. They all knew of the kingdoms and lands, including those of the Jews, that Rome had conquered. It had been proven time and time again, that there was no force on earth as strong as the legion and no kingdom had yet stood against them.

Balthazar answered, "I wish to avoid conflict with Rome. They have never taken a liking to our kingdoms, so I am happy with that but we must continue to search for truth. We will tread carefully and above all, wisely. Caspar?"

Caspar thoughtfully nodded once. "I agree. We will follow the star. We will maintain we are on a pilgrimage and are traveling to greet the newborn King, I don't honestly think the Romans know of him yet and they aren't looking for Him. They may hear of Him from their pet Jews, but they won't believe He can hurt them.

"And they probably wouldn't listen if a prophet told them the King of the Jews had been born, they don't believe the prophecies and are entirely ignorant of things in the heavens", Balthazar said.

"So, we agree to go forward; and find the Newborn before the Romans get word of Him and we have to deal with them. Meanwhile we have to travel through their provinces but we will continue to consult the prophecies and His star as to where we will find Him and what to do then.

Week 6

Poisoned Caravan

B althazar looked up as Japheth reported, "We should arrive at the oasis tonight if the sands haven't shifted so much that our maps are off."

The caravan continued west into the dark; but instead of the quietness and measured movement of the animals in the moonlight, everyone was alert and excited about the refreshment to come at the wells.

Japheth finally approached the magi atop their camels with welcome news, "My lords, the maps are still correct—water and comfort is ahead at the oasis. Riders have returned and report there is no other caravan there; we can stop and refresh ourselves."

"Well done. Shadrach?"

"Here my lord. Our soldiers are already there securing it for us, there is no threat. Also, I have reinforced those caring for our animals as we get closer and the cattle smell the water. We are protected."

As the caravan paused at the top of a sand hill, the valley in front of them was lit by the amazing star. The oasis was clearly visible directly west of them, palm trees stood over patches of grass and low shrubs, large pools of water sparkled, and one could almost smell the ripe figs.

The caravan arrived and settled among the grass and water. Work began immediately on repairing and cleaning ropes, ties, and other damage received in the attack. Herds were carefully watered, fed and then let free near the stock pools, clothing was washed, and water jugs were filled to capacity.

As work continued, music was soon heard. People were relaxing from the constant travel and friends gathered at different wells and ponds. Figs and dates were gathered from the many trees, youngsters laughingly searched for wild berries and little children collected cow patties, dry manure, for the camp fires.

Kitchen workers fanned out to search for wild grain because it was usually plentiful at the oasis. Grain was found at watering sites because it is often dropped from earlier travelers and then grows well in the sun and abundant water. However, oases are dangerous because everyone wants access to water and food and there are some who will attack and kill for it. There has never been any one group that per-manently lives at these oases, and there were always things left behind.

Finding water and food in the immense desert is always something to celebrate. It is well known that only those with knowledge and guidance from maps can find their long way and survive in the heat of the day and the extreme cold each night. There are many caravans that leave their homes, disap-pear into the desert, and are never seen again.

The magi dismounted from their camels and collected their parchments, and as they looked to the immense star that dominated the heavens, they quietly spoke of the next step, and of course, the Newborn.

"Look again; the star has stopped its movement. It waits for us! The Lord of heaven has surely sent it to show us the way to His child, He continues to guide our way. But to know that all of heaven does his bidding and that He thinks of us is beyond my imagination," exclaimed Balthazar.

The three men were quiet for a long while and then Caspar spoke, "Whatever He wants of us, this newborn King of kings, I am ready to follow Him. He controls heaven and He must be coming to spread His domain to us here on earth. How should we worship Him?"

"He comes to change the world and you know that means we are supporting a king that will bring revolutionary changes, one who is intent on replacing the law as His people know it. This may go badly for our own positions," stated Balthazar.

"He won't be popular, especially with His own people."

"No, He won't. But He is Lord and King." Caspar continued, "I want to be part of His kingdom, I want to be part of His change."

And Melchior, the elder, who had seen so many things and still thirsted for knowledge added, "Yes, there must be a place for us. Balthazar, what do you say?"

"Yes, there is a place for us; we are bringing treasure and goods and don't forget, we could provide an army for Him. What more could He or any king want?"

Melchior looked at Balthazar, realizing that he didn't get the bigger picture yet, "More, I think He wants more."

The caravan rested and restocked food and supplies. After a full night and another day of rest, the star continued its journey as the sun dipped low and shadows were stretching across the sands.

Following, the caravan gathered itself and started its westward journey also. The herds were refreshed and moved grudgingly away from the grasses and the camels lined up for their long walk through the night.

Japheth reported, "We should be able to cover almost halfway to the next wells. They aren't an oasis but it will afford what we need."

Then a returning soldier dismounted and was immediately at Shadrach's side. "Sir, I've just returned from checking on the scouts, four of the soldiers who have gone ahead are sick. I brought back three of them; they couldn't even stay on their animals."

"What is wrong with them? Soldiers don't get sick. They do their duty."

"Sir, I don't know, they look bad, even in the dark and their tongues are swelling so much they can't breathe. They are dying!"

Send a company out to reinforce the other scouts and secure us with another one in case this is some sort of attack. Stop the caravan!"

Shadrach strode to the magi, "My lords, there is something wrong ahead with my soldiers. I have a report that they are dying, I have sent a company out to secure them and added another company to protect us. I'm not sure what this is; I have stopped the caravan."

Melchior then turned to Balthazar, "Their tongues are swelling? It sounds like poison. Capt Shadrach, we will look at these soldiers. Until we know more, see that no one eats anything else until it is checked carefully."

Melchior removed a camel-hair pouch that was hanging from the pommel of his saddle, "Is this happening to anyone other than the scouts?" The question was soon answered when a human shriek followed by a wail was heard somewhere in the middle of the line of camels.

The magi were inspecting the sick as others continued to collapse. "Two of our camel drivers are sick and they are gasping for breath! And where is the water-bearer?" Illya looked pale and queasy as a half a dozen more workers were found to be sick and looked to be dying or were dead.

Melchior straightened after he and Balthazar had examined the drivers and the soldiers that had been returned from the front of the line, two were dead and one was critical.

He went over to the next one and bent low. The soldier would have been dead already but he was young and strong. His chest looked almost unable to move so he was struggling hard to breath and sweat was pouring off of him as he fought to stay alive. He had opened his mouth to breath; the wheezing was horrible and his tongue was swollen and blue. The soldiers guarding the camp's perimeter looked at each other, they all knew what dying looked and sounded like.

"I know this smell of almonds and I have seen this before; it is poison. Look at the frothing at the mouth, he can't breathe because everything is paralyzed but I have no medicine for this. It kills so fast! I can try one more thing, but it is just a faint hope—it all depends on how much was he ate."

The young soldier continued to struggle to breathe but he was losing strength fast and his face was completely white and his lips were dark blue. He was fully conscious but no longer able to make any sounds except for the terrible gurgling coming from his swollen throat.

Melchior remained at the soldier's side. He was trying to remember all that he knew about this poison. His eyes suddenly brightened, he grew still and briefly looked down. He had obviously made a decision and swiftly pulled the soldier's knife from his belt. As he raised it to the soldier's neck, the boy's eyes grew wide and unbelieving. Seeing his response, Melchior placed his hand over the boy's eyes and quickly buried the tip of the knife in the front of his neck.

Out spewed blood and gore, and as Melchior slipped in the mess, he called, "Hand me a tube, something that won't collapse. Anything will do. He can still breathe on his own, but needs help, but it has to be now!"

Everyone scrambled to look for a tube. They ransacked the area and they could clearly hear the soldier's breathing begin to be labored again. It could be heard; it seemed, throughout the entire caravan. Melchior called out again and this time urgently, "Hurry, please. His time is very short without a miracle."

The search became frantic. Caspar looked over and saw the sparkle of Melchior's large ring on his index finger. It was of course, hollow, at least three inches long, and a perfect tube.

"Here it is." He lifted Melchior's hand and raised his eyebrows. Melchior smiled briefly and slipped off his ring into Caspar's waiting hand. He turned back to the soldier, who no longer was completely conscious, to calculate if it would work, "Caspar, I think it will fit!" They both looked at the ring and

Melchior looked once again at Caspar as he dipped it into a cleansing wash.

Those in the tent grimaced as Melchior pushed the ring into the gaping hole in the soldier's neck. When he did, the soldier let out a great cough that caused more globs of mucus and blood to fly out through the ring and clear his airway. Almost immediately, his breathing became easier.

Everyone in the tent stared at him, as his color became normal; and at the jewel-encrusted ring, buried deep in his neck, twinkling with every breath.

Week 7

More Death

"M elchior, what is this"?
Poison and if you can keep a victim from choking
in the first minutes, they have a chance. We need to find out
where this came from and stop it or we all will be in this condition. Start with the water and food supplies."

Shadrach stood at the bedside of the soldier and turned as
one of his men came in. Reporting, the man spoke softly while
at first averting his eyes from his poisoned coworker, then
hesitantly glancing, he apparently seemed to be mesmerized.
The patient was stable and doing better but not a pretty sight.
The soldiers were used to the gore of battle but now they were
wondering if they would even be aware if they were the next
target of this invisible attacker.

Shadrach dismissed the scout and turned, "My lords, two
herders have been found dead, four soldiers are dead, several
others are slightly ill and maybe this one will live. He stared
straight at Keenai, Balthazar's personal chef and overseer of
food supplies "The caravan seems to have been poisoned.
Since food or drink is suspected, I believe we have found the
one responsible."

Balthazar frowned as he stood up and interrupted him,
"We will move this discussion to another area. Illya!"

"My lord, both royal parlors are available."

Sebastian, Balthazar's trusted advisor walked with him, "I have already begun an investigation, preliminary reports point to the grain at the oasis. Those who didn't pick the fresh grain, but gathered it from the ground are the ones that are choking."

Once inside a private tent Keenai protested, "You're wrong; everyone has eaten bread made from that grain."

"Yes, but the difference is that the bread was baked, the poison is neutralized when it is heated. Some people ate the tops off the grain that was growing and others simply found piles of grain on the ground.

"There are no reports that it is the water? There were many wells there and of course, the standing water."

"No reliable ones, so I don't think so."

"So my men have been poisoned by their food!" Shadrach turned swiftly to shout at Keenai and in response, several of Balthazar's guards moved closer. Shadrach was mad; he had just lost some of his soldiers and more could succumb. "We need to find out what is really happening because even if you are too stupid, I realize that my soldiers are the ones who are falling. Few others have been as affected."

Keenai was now on the offense; he was in charge of food and water during caravan journeys and took his responsibility very seriously. He grew red in the face and yelled back, "That's because your soldiers are so lazy that they just picked up grain that was lying on the ground—in fact, they poisoned themselves. Our food supplies are not poison!"

Keenai had walked over to Shadrach, seemingly unaware that he faced a man that was personally grieving these deaths and was also angry and frustrated that there was no enemy to fight. He hated to have to accept losses without being able to strike back, to defeat the enemy.

Shadrach bellowed, "Don't you even think my soldiers poisoned themselves! Aren't you in charge of the food? Why didn't you make sure everything was fit to eat? It's your fault."

Keenai raised his fist as he escalated the shouting match and with that, Shadrach grabbed his wrist, twisted it behind him and kicked him down. The fight started.

The guards stood between Balthazar and the men on the ground, they unsheathed short swords but they were relaxed they as they watched their commander easily outwrestle his opponent. Soon Balthazar's deep voice resonated, "Stop—separate and stand up." He had seen heated arguments and fights between soldiers in the barracks and was aware they could get out of hand quickly. However, they were often easily stopped, tempers cooled and then everyone would go back to their jobs.

His voice had authority and could be heard over the noise. Shadrach heard the order and responded immediately; but Keenai was still hot in the fight and his momentum carried him forward. He fell onto Shadrach as he was standing up. "Get off of me, you snake," he said as he jabbed back with his elbow and turned to watch as Keenai fell off of his back.

Balthazar had sat down and Sebastian spoke to all, "We have lost friends but we need to come together to find what is attacking us all." Keenai had not moved.

One of the guards knelt down and turned him over, his nose and face was bleeding and he started to convulse. "Commander!" he called as he looked over at Shadrach as everyone in the tent looked down at Keenai.

Balthazar and Sebastian were instantly at his side, "He has a brain injury, let's get a blanket or something under him."

Then everything happened at once, Balthazar's personal guards surrounded their mage, others scrambled out of the way. Melchior was already supporting Keenai as he lay awkwardly on his back, his nose was bleeding and blood was seeping from an ear. He was unconscious and it was apparent that death was just a few moments away.

Melchior was trying to staunch the flow of blood from his nose "Keenai, listen to me. I don't want to put too much pressure on your nose because it will cause you terrible pain and even more damage. Can you hear me?"

Turning to Balthazar, "He has suffered a brain injury, I can't believe this has to do with the poison."

Keenai was finally still and let out a loud groan. Melchior shook his head sadly, 'If you hurt, I can give you something, it will send you quietly to your death, if you desire."

A moment later, Keenai opened his eyes. He couldn't move and he slowly responded in a slurred weak voice, "No, the pain is going away."

In a few minutes he continued in a much quieter voice, "Please tell me my lord, I have listened to you talk about your search. I have wondered; I really just want to know about the Newborn you are seeking, "do you think He is really. . .the. . . . . Messiah?" And with that last whispered question still on his lips, Keenai died, still looking up hopefully at Melchior.

Shadrach stared in disbelief: "I didn't mean to kill him, we were arguing!" A very grim Madai took charge of him, checked to see if he had other weapons on his person, then pausing to look back at Balthazar, ordered the guards to bind him and remove him from the tent.

"My lords, the laws are very clear about what to do with a person who kills another during caravan travel. They don't require a trial or consideration; the guilty one should be left to die in the desert.

Balthazar had walked over to where Shadrach still stood in confusion. He longed to just tell everyone to go back to what they were doing and to just find the poison so everyone could be safe. But he knew with certainty that not everyone was safe. Not only was he king but he was the law also and he prided himself on ruling according to laws, not on favoritism or on a whim.

Shadrach was a trusted friend, a loyal subject and a soldier of the realm. Balthazar hung his head; he was crushed with the thought. Shadrach was above all, a good and beloved friend.

He knew what he had done however, and bowed his head and quietly acknowledged his king, but did not ask for leniency, "Balthazar, my king, I beg your pardon and I understand my sentence. I am guilty of murdering one of your subjects."

Balthazar grasped his forearm, just as they had done for years when they were soldiers together and they stood like that for a short time. Then, "Keep him confined for now. We know what we have to do. Both men have served my house for generations."

Madai escorted the bound Shadrach out of the tent and Balthazar was quiet. Caspar took a breath, "Let us have Keenai's body cared for and then we will discuss what we need to do."

Illya supervised the transfer of the body and cleaning up. Madai, reported back, clearly grieving, and asked to be placed in charge of the arrangements. Then he again pledged his loyalty and support to Balthazar's house, then took up leadership of the soldiers.

He had worked closely with Shadrach and enjoyed the camaraderie; he knew he would be missed. He checked on the guards that were present and then quietly asked, "Illya, you were here. What happened? We are soldiers, we live with death every day, and we expect to die in battle and not be lured into a stupid argument in our master's tent."

"Madai, we don't know where death will find us. Shadrach believed he was in battle. He was fighting to find the cause of the poisonings, he was fighting for all of us—just because he wasn't riding a warhorse and galloping into the frenzy of battle doesn't mean he wasn't soldiering. Tell your soldiers that he is still a hero; and yes, Keenai is dead but not because Shadrach planned it. Death is fickle and often surprises us with his choices.

"So be careful about what you are saying. I'll tell you this once and this will be the end of it. There was an argument, and they went down to the ground. Lord Balthazar commanded them to stop and rise; Shadrach rolled away first and because he was so quick to obey, Keenai was the only one still in the fight and that's why Shadrach didn't attack him. He just pushed him.

So, say what you need to in order to inform and comfort your troops but don't start anything. Shadrach will be sentenced according to Lord Balthazar's requests and his laws.

Just don't be a problem or you will find yourself left behind with him."

In another part of the caravan Caspar asked, "How are the others?"

Balthazar asked, "You mean the others that are sick, the ones that are dead or the one to be sentenced?"

Melchior answered, "First things first. There have been no new deaths, those that are ill are still ill and seem to be recovering slowly. Our dead are being cared for. And as for the one to be sentenced, Balthazar, you know the laws better than any of us. Anyone who attacks and injures another person to the point of death, especially when traveling in caravan is left behind in the desert. His legs can be cut so he can't walk, or he can be left on his own with or without water. Anyway, it's best to follow those laws, unless you want to address something else?"

All three men stood together, no one liked this but they were determined to be united. If there was some custom, however that they could follow that would allow mercy for Shadrach, they would find it and be much happier.

"No, I understand the importance of laws in my kingdom. But, how I wish he hadn't done it! He is a good man, I know it! His family has served mine for generations and now, because of a moment of anger."

Balthazar pounded his fist on the table. "But enough! I want no further harm to come to him from us and he is to have as much water as a skin can hold, but he will be left behind and hopefully God will have mercy on him and kill him quickly."

Illya had been listening, "My lord, everything has been done. Everyone will assemble this evening for the sentence to be pronounced and then we leave this place. We will be ready."

Balthazar said nothing; he was sitting at his desk and looking out onto the open porch of his tent seemingly into the far distance. He was sad and agitated, and felt all alone. Illya peered up at him again as he bowed away and noticed the ancient scrolls in Balthazar's hands that he had kept twisting around and around were now shredded beyond repair.

~~~~~~~~~~~~~~~~~~~

The magi sat on three sculpted thrones; each was unique and beautifully made, befitting their royal ranks They were clothed in majestic purple, gold, and priestly green, each held a jeweled scepter of their authority and their heads were adorned with crowns of their kingdoms. This day, they sat in judgment.

Balthazar looked a long time at Shadrach before speaking in a voice that easily carried across the silenced caravan.

"This one is found guilty of murder, murder of a member of his own caravan. The sentence shall be: He is to be shunned from the caravan. He will be left behind on his own in the desert. He will be given one skin of water. May God have mercy on him."

Then the magi rose from their thrones one by one, Balthazar last. Shadrach finally looked up at him, nodded his head and then was returned to a holding tent.

Law had prohibited Shadrach from speaking. He hung his head and knew he was guilty; he was so ashamed. He loved Balthazar and realized he deserved this sentence, and was even grateful for the skin of water, but also knew he had hoped to be killed quickly. He knew how hot the desert got in the daytime and how cold it was each night. To live, he would have to survive the packs of starving animals that tracked food at night, he would have to avoid the bands of thieves and cutthroats that roamed the desert, and he would have to find water and shelter from the cold night desert that would let him live until he burned alive in the heat of the sun.

As the sun dipped below the hills of sand, the caravan moved out quietly, in mourning for its losses. No one said anything or looked back, but all were aware of the figure left behind with a single skin of water.

As for Shadrach, he was ready to face death. He had been left behind with a full skin of water and a thin cloak to cover him in the coming night. During the day he had thought time and time again of the stupidity of his actions and the last words Keenai spoke. They seemed to comfort him.

Week 8

The Golden Messenger

A s the sun finally disappeared behind the towering hills of sand and shrub the cold immediately set in. The beckoning star resumed its westward glide through the heavens and the caravan followed. The magi were riding atop their camels and wrapped long winding weather-weight mantles around themselves to keep warm as they gathered close to speak of events. Slowly a quiet, calm settled over the sad travelers.

Caspar had returned to his star maps and scriptures, gazing between them and the heavens, mumbling to himself. Melchior was checking the lists of supplies and giving directions to Tsion, who had been given Keenai's duties. Balthazar's camel had moved slightly ahead of the others, and then came Caspar followed by Melchior as each went about their business. The desert was so still at night that hushed voices, muffled footsteps and the caravan's movements were all easily heard.

Balthazar was rereading messages from home, smiling at the small talk and often his face became sad as he read about concerns. He thought about his quest for the newborn king, about leaving his loved ones and how he missed them so much. He started when he noticed one of camels had come almost even with his and the rider, unrecognizable in the dark, seemed to be looking at him intently.

The rider spoke, "Since the day you humbled yourself and searched for God, He has heard you and has had compassion on you. Balthazar, what is your most fervent wish?"

"Wisdom, truth", Balthazar replied without hesitation, and then belatedly realized that this was someone he didn't know. "Who are you?"

Instantly, the "person" became golden and as bright as day, causing the sand around them to reflect the light so the entire area shone. As Balthazar stared, open-mouthed, he was able to see that the golden being was clothed in garments that seemed to shimmer and move in power. He was powerfully built and sat astride a pure white animal that had the beauty and strength of a horse and the apparent power of a camel.

Balthazar was overwhelmed, his jaw hung loosely as he sat motionless. He couldn't take his eyes from the being.

"I come in the name of the Most High God. He is your Creator, Sustainer, and Lover of your soul; and now He has given you a redeemer. The Redeemer is the Newborn that you seek and He surely is the King of kings and Lord of lords. He is the Son of God Almighty and He is Perfection sent to earth to save all mankind.

"He is the One that you read of in the ancient scriptures. He is wisdom and Creator of all truth; He is able to save all who call on Him."

As he sat in silence Balthazar would probably have fallen off of his camel, if he had not been seated so snugly in the saddle; instead and without thought, he raised his hands in praise of God while he bowed his face downward. He knew about messengers and he himself also had those who did his bidding; but this being was so different from any other messenger that he had ever seen.

He wondered briefly if he was going to die and shook so hard in amazement that his teeth chattered and he could barely speak, even though it was apparent that the messenger was waiting for him to respond.

So he just spoke without thought, straight from his heart, "The Divine King whose star we follow is the Prophesied One? What would He have me do?" he asked clumsily.

The golden one slowly inclined his head in agreement, "Well said King Balthazar. The Lord of lords has summoned you to His birth for His own reasons, and you are to follow His star as it guides you to the destination. There will be tragedies and sorrows along the way, but trust that you are being guided.

You will soon come to know that you are traveling toward Jerusalem. When you inquire of King Herod about the birth of the One called King of the Jews, he will want to find out more and you will be invited to stay overnight in his palace. There is danger for you there so refuse and continue on your way immediately. Settle your caravan out of the town because from there you are to continue the journey."

The messenger, having finished his task, disappeared as Balthazar looked up into his radiant face.

Energized, Balthazar straightened his back and called over to his friends, "Melchior, Caspar, the messenger! Did you see the amazing messenger?"

However, Caspar didn't even raise his head as he replied, "A messenger has arrived from where? Have him brought to us and we will give him food and water as he shares the news."

Melchior had drawn close enough to see Balthazar's face, and it became apparent that only Balthazar had seen the heavenly messenger, "Look, look at your face, it shines! You have seen God!"

Week 9

Angels Proclaim Him

C aspar brought his camel closer, over to where Melchior was staring at Balthazar. It was true, Balthazar seemed to be glowing, and his sun-darkened skin even lightened the area around him.

"What did you hear? What did He say?"

Balthazar was eager to share the good news. Everyone in the households and in the lands where the magi reigned knew of the mighty king that the scriptures and the heavens foretold, because the prophecies were common knowledge.

Even though these people from the east didn't see him as *their* king, they respected royalty. Some of them were Jewish and most were raised on battle stories of David, the warrior king, and the powerful works of the Almighty God that he worshipped. They shared stories of how all of the king's enemies were crushed, and unbelievable treasures from their cities and lands had been given to David, the favored one of his Lord God.

"City of David! We are going to Jerusalem! He will be born there?" exclaimed Caspar.

"The star is guiding us to Jerusalem?"

"Yes, but the angel told us that we were not to stay in Jerusalem but to continue our journey. We are to present ourselves to Herod."

Melchior shook his head, "Not a pleasant idea because not only did the angel tell us Herod is not to be trusted, but my family has had dealings with him when he wanted to detain our ambassador to his court. Beware of him; he is crazy, he wouldn't hesitate to imprison, torture, or kill us all and he isn't particular about needing an excuse. He has been given a lot of authority by the Rome and as long as he stays their puppet, he won't worry about how he treats other kingdoms."

Balthazar protested, "He can't harm us, what would he say to our households? And to our countries? We just can't disappear."

"Yes, he can and he wouldn't care too much about the consequences except he does care about what Rome thinks. In our case, I'm sure that he knows about our countries' treaties and he is smart enough to know he would need a good reason to delay or harm us. He has the might of Rome behind him in order to control his country so we have to be careful how we present ourselves as we enter his court; and not be too obvious that we are not completely open with him."

"I heard the messenger clearly, and we will obey. We will present ourselves to find out where in Jerusalem that the newborn King has been born and we will leave as soon as we get the answer we need."

Caspar asked, "What do you think it means? It has been written that He will be found lying in a manger."

"Maybe it means He has been given power over life, since the manger may mean "life-giving". A newborn King lying in a golden manger in the palace in the City of David, what else could it mean?" asked Balthazar and Melchior.

"Why do you say golden manger and a palace, which palace?" countered Caspar. "He certainly won't be at Herod's palace so where else would he be in Jerusalem? Certainly his family will have been hidden him carefully from his enemies."

"Who would know where a hidden newborn King is, the one proclaimed by heavenly angels? And he said City of David, but certainly not a real stable?" asked Melchior. However, a new thought was beginning to form.

Balthazar said, "But first, we will build an altar here honoring King David's God from whom the holy messengers were sent to speak to us."

"Yes, but what is His name? We don't even know Him. He is calling us to greet his Son but what does He want from us?" questioned Melchior.

As the three discussed making an altar of stones in honor of the god they didn't know, they found they had more questions than answers about Him.

Finally they agreed on one thing—it should be a well-made altar with a single offering placed upon it. Then they questioned, "What offering does this god want?"

"Let's not offend Him. We don't know anything about His requirements however, and if His Son will be King of the Jews, then we must think of the many laws that he demands they live by. And there are many."

Religious laws and history were important to the magi. They ruled their own countries in accordance with them and much of their own power was given to them by these laws. "So this means we offer a lamb or something like that? And what of the ceremony? Do we use music, or do we intone supplications? More importantly, what is this King's name? "

Caspar said, "This God is different from the other gods that we know of, we can't just look at what others have done, pick out an animal and then say 'Unknown God; here, have a goat.'"

The star had stopped during the angel's proclamations and the magi's discussions as if it patiently waited for them to come to a decision. Caspar had been consulting with a Jewish scholar who accompanied him; they both were looking at a scroll. He nodded his head and said, "I know. . ."

The others came close as Caspar eagerly explained his theory. And they got to work.

Later on, the star shone over the desert with renewed intensity as it continued its westward journey. The people in the caravan were still talking about the night's visitor as they went about their work and the camels slowly started moving.

As the caravan left, a simple, beautifully-made altar stood behind. A curl of smoke from the fragrant offering of first-harvested grain mixed with precious oils rose toward the heavens. Balthazar gazed at it and felt a deep peace inside. He imagined he could see all of his prayers for their journey, his family, those in the caravan, and even for Shadrach who he had condemned, rising up with the smoke. He smiled with approval at the name that was carved in the altar, "I AM".

Week 10

Visitors

T he shepherd boy had stood very still by his flock at the arrival of the angel and heard his proclamations of the coming of the newborn King. It was true, he couldn't really see anymore, the injury to his head and eyes left him able to see only the difference between light and darkness. Nothing more. But it seemed that his hearing and awareness was heightened and because of that he could still care for the sheep.

He had known the angel was there before anyone else. He was walking on the side of the hill calling the sheep as he followed the bright star in the western sky. There was a sudden golden light right in front of him and he stopped short and immediately raised his staff. The lamb in his arms bleated as the boy's arms tensed, ready to defend against the threat.

"Greetings! Do not be afraid shepherd; I bring you joyful tidings from God Most High. The Holy Infant will soon be born and He will seek and find the lost. You will understand this and the Father wants you to know of His great love for you. You are important to him and He has a place for you within His kingdom."

The boy knew truth when he heard it and wasn't afraid. He could only see the golden light from the angel and nothing else but he knelt down with the lamb still in his arms and answered the angel from his heart. "I want to learn more about the Father. I promise to follow His Son, the Newborn

King." He didn't ask for anything for himself. "But forgive me; I don't know why the Most High God would love me. How can I be of any use to Him? I am small and weak." Could he dare to believe that there was a place for him in his kingdom? Yes, he would follow the Newborn.

"You have chosen to turn from bitterness and to have a loving heart, full of trust. The Father values your love above many, many things."

The angel lingered, looking at the boy and then he extended his hand and held it on the boy's head. The shepherd knew he was being blessed. He felt a terrific, enveloping love that made his hard life that was now full of loneliness and pain, recede into the background. The love became all important, his sight didn't return, but the pain in his head and the loneliness in his heart went away.

Week 11

Cast Out

A t the same time the angel was blessing the shepherd boy, a solitary figure stumbled along at the side of a sand dune far behind the caravan. He was weak and at the end of his water, and was trying to soak up the heat that was rapidly leaving the sand as the night progressed. He didn't know why he was still alive.

Shadrach had survived the scorching sun during the long day and now he was shivering in the chill of the night, each breeze stinging his sunburned skin. He was thirsty and cold; he hurt from his sunburned skin and eyes, and could not remember ever being so alone. Yet he knew his punishment was just, he was a murderer and judgment had been passed, if only he could go back to that morning before all of this happened.

Shadrach's legs slowly buckled under him and he landed on his back. He was groggy and at first tried to get back on his knees but his legs just wouldn't work anymore.

"Hello! Hello?. . .Is there anyone there?" He thought he heard people talking.

"I'm crazy. That's all; there is no one out here. Why would there be people out in the desert at night without torches? It's too dark to see anything."

Again he heard a voice so he desperately tried again, "Is anyone there?"

But to himself he thought, "These aren't people that I'm hearing, it has to be approaching animals."

He had seen groups of predators follow caravans at a distance to feed on the trash or weakened animals. He knew that they hunted the desert at night and probably had been stalking him. Now they found him and they knew they could wait. They would stay just out of sight until he was so weak he couldn't put up much of a fight, and then they would approach and devour him.

Time went by, how much he didn't know. He heard steps and rustlings as they got closer, so he knew his death was near. He decided to raise his head to face his death.

His eyes were deceiving him! Oh, how terrible that this mirage looked so real! Across from him sat a clean and well-dressed man who quickly finished making a small fire that immediately began warming Shadrach's shivering body. He paused and looked at him expectantly and then offered him a gourd of water.

Shadrach didn't move, he waited for the vision to vanish and for the dark to return. The man continued to sit there with a slight smile on his face and answered his thoughts. "No, I am real Shadrach; here, drink while you warm yourself."

Shadrach wanted to hesitate, but the light and the warmth of the fire was real and he desperately wanted the water. He didn't realize that the man had answered his unspoken thoughts. His unsteady hold on the full gourd caused some of the water to splash onto the back of his hand and to the ground; he looked down at it and paused only a second and then thirstily drank, then asked for more.

The man already was dipping out more water from the jug at his side and steadied him, "Drink more slowly this time. There is plenty."

The man's arm was strong. He was not a mirage and the fire warmed Shadrach as the water quenched his thirst and cleared his mind. "This was just not done! No one comes upon an outcast in the desert and gives him comfort. Those left behind are abandoned as punishment for the most serious offenses, this man would know that. Why had he rescued him?"

"You know my name! Why are you here?" He thought that maybe this man was somehow related to Keenai and had come to enjoy the sight of him dying. This time when he heard the man's answer, he was aware he was answering his thoughts. The man was ordinary looking, but his eyes were full of empathy and his voice echoed in Shadrach's empty heart.

"I come in the name of the Almighty God, and have been sent to encourage you Shadrach. Not condemn you."

Shadrach's mouth dropped open, even as his mind tried to understand who or what he was seeing in front of him.

"Fear not, the Lord God knows your heart and even though you have greatly sinned by murdering another man, He has seen your broken heart and has heard your prayers. He is the One to whom you call on, He is the All Powerful One and He has delighted in bringing you to Himself."

Shadrach had gotten to his knees and bowed his head in the presence of the messenger of the Almighty One. The angel's message sent a great light into his heart and chased away all darkness and loneliness and even though he was still a condemned man, cast out by the world, and alone in the desert, he had hope.

The angel continued, "Almighty God is with you. His Son will come into the world, to save it from its sins. I bring you these glad tidings for they are for all people and He wants you to know that He has a plan for you, Shadrach.

You are to be a messenger for Him to carry the Good News. So arise, your strength has returned; and as your faith grows, your grace will be renewed each day. You are to take no provisions, but you are to start walking now. Walk west toward the star and you will find pilgrims in the distance. Accept their hospitality."

Shadrach knew he had gone from sure death to the start of a different type of life. He knew he didn't deserve any of this but he knew he had been given another chance. He had a reason to live, and the Almighty God to serve. He was no longer hungry, thirsty, or tired and he was still kneeling as he raised his arms to heaven. He praised the Almighty God who saw him and chose to save him, and simply asked to know Him more.

As he was praying, he felt the angel also kneel close by and he heard a great loving voice in his heart, "I am the Lord God Almighty, the great 'I AM.'"

Shadrach raised his head, "Lord God Almighty, you must know all about me but in your mercy you have chosen me to serve you. I want to know you and your Son and to serve you with all of my heart."

He didn't know how long he prayed and thanked God but when he opened his eyes, there was no angel, no fire, and no sign of water in a gourd. He was strong and clear-minded, however. He got to his feet and started west, following the guiding star, more certain of himself that he had ever been.

Week 12

Balthazar is Ill

The caravan arrived at a small oasis in the early dawn, about an hour before the sun would be rising. Even after the exciting night, everyone tended to the menial jobs they were assigned that kept them safe and alive during the long trip. The household was secured and then the provisions were checked. After tents were set up and the flocks and camels were cared for, there was time to eat and watch the sun rise as the magi made notes in their journals and consulted with their advisors and messengers arrived.

Meanwhile, riders left the camp to scout ahead, and look outs and soldiers kept guard as most of the household soon slept under shelters that allowed breezes to sweep over the sleeper but kept out the burning sun. Still, it was hot, dangerously hot to be out; no one would choose to be up traveling in the desert during the day.

Balthazar finished writing in his journal about the events of the night.

He sighed deeply and Melchior, sitting close by, didn't even look up from his scrolls as he said "It's true. The boy's wounds look different. The evidence of his injuries is still there, but the wounds somehow are healthier, they are definitely not infected and the skin has almost closed. No more redness or draining, but he can't see either. Moreover, the greatest healing has been in his heart—he isn't afraid of his life without sight, he has *peace*."

He continued, "And how many of us have peace? Do you, my friend?"

Balthazar fidgeted and then started softly, "I should, shouldn't I? I have seen and I believe the heavenly messengers, but I am always worried. I worry that I may make a mistake in my relationship with the Newborn and thereby destroy my kingdom; I worry about my wife and family at home without me. I worry that I made a mistake with Shadrach. I worry all the time and I don't know when I last slept or ate."

Caspar tucked his scrolls into a fabric bag and turned to Balthazar, wanting to give him a measure of peace. "Melchior is right. We are on the journey of our lives. We are led daily by a guiding star, messengers sent by Almighty God have acknowledged us and proclaimed the truth of the newborn we seek, and we traveling toward our goal. Don't you think that if the Newborn can affect all of these things and then miraculously see to the needs of a shepherd boy that we can be sure of the path that we are following?"

Balthazar scrubbed his face with his hands, "No, I mean, yes. I am just uneasy. I am all right; I'm going to walk around. Please, get some sleep."

Caspar rise and started to follow after he saw he was actually going outside, "Where are you going? The sun has already reached the horizon and it will be very hot soon. Here, let me walk with you."

"No need", responded Balthazar as he skittered ahead of him, "I just need some time by myself. I'll walk a little to stretch, and then I'll go to my tent to sleep."

Caspar stopped and shrugged his shoulders, "All right. Clear your mind, trust and have faith."

Balthazar pushed aside the tasseled opening of the silk tent and left. Caspar turned to Melchior, "He is so worried and seems to be getting worse. I don't know why."

Melchior's eyes were still on Balthazar as he stumbled away, followed by a very sleepy Illya. "Every day he becomes more anxious, I have noticed that he walks and walks each morning when most of us are sleeping. Look at Illya also; he is worn out and can barely keep his eyes open."

"We should watch him; I don't think he looks well."

Balthazar hadn't told anyone that his anxiety was so bad that he was sleeping only minutes each day. He was getting confused and now could only eat when he was so sleepy that his mind wasn't working. He didn't know what exactly it was that he was so worried about, but it had to be related to the same awful vision he continued to have.

"I know I should confide in Melchior about the vision, maybe he can help me to understand it. But I'm afraid that it is telling me what I don't want to hear, that I will lose everything. He raised his head and paused, the vision unfolded in front of him.

In his vision, he clearly saw himself bowing, then removing his own crown and then going to a knee to offer it to an unknown king on a throne. On a knee, in the way that a conquered king gives his kingdom to the victor before he is killed! It had to mean that he would be dead and his kingdom gone. What about his family? Who could help him?

Balthazar had the gifts of vision and prophecy; but these were burdens as well. Sometimes he felt he would be better off without the knowledge his visions brought him. His teachers often reminded him of his responsibilities because he had these abilities and this worried him. He had episodes of these types of worries in his life, but they had all passed.

This one wasn't passing, but getting steadily worse. Would he have to return home? How long before he was just unable to continue? He wished he knew what to do about himself; wasn't there some medicine? Or some soothing words that his mind could understand? He walked with his head down, not looking where he was going and vaguely he heard Illya's voice but he didn't understand him. He was just too tired.

"Majesty please let me help you. You are very close to the ravine here and the sand is too soft to hold us. Majesty, please allow me to help you back to your tent; wouldn't you like to rest now?"

Illya was not aware that Balthazar was in such a state. He was very worried about his master's health, he had seen him anxious and depressed before, but Balthazar had always found ways to pull himself out of it. This time was different and he was becoming a danger to himself and others.

Balthazar didn't answer and was walking by himself several steps in front of Illya along the edge of the camp. He rounded some tall barrels of water used for the flocks and slipped. His arms flailed in the air as he slid off the side of the sand dune. He made no sound.

"Oh no! Help!" Illya called and he ran forward to grab him but only caught the edge of his silken robe and it slipped through his hands. Balthazar rolled down the embankment, throwing sand in the air. Illya launched himself off of the edge of the ravine, landing in the shifting soft sands behind Balthazar as he continued to roll. Balthazar finally lay still at the bottom of the ravine. He was dizzy and nauseated from the violent fall and roll, and he was bruised and scraped up but he just didn't care.

Illya landed by his side and immediately was brushing the sand out of his face and straightening his garments that had wrapped tightly around him as he had rolled. "My lord, please talk to me! Are you hurt?"

Faces appeared at the top of the ravine and soldiers quickly were seen making an orderly descent with water and a litter among them.

Melchior and Caspar's worried faces were soon at his side. "Balthazar! Don't move! Are you all right? Anything broken?"

Illya looked up and babbled, "My lords, I'm sorry. I couldn't help him; he just didn't look up at all when he was walking. I just couldn't stop him. I warned him, he didn't hear."

Melchior and Caspar were immediately at Balthazar's side but Melchior was looking at Illya. "Has he slept at all? When is the last time he ate; I mean, really ate a meal?"

"My lord, he doesn't sleep anymore. He just doesn't sleep and as for eating; no, he has no interest in anything."

Caspar moved Illya away from Balthazar's immediate side, "You can tell me Illya, I know he needs help. Do you think he may hurt himself?"

Thankful that his fears were out in the open Illya nodded his head forcefully, "Yes, my lord. I fear for him."

Meanwhile Balthazar had said nothing and really just wanted to go away. He closed his eyes. He was hastily checked for broken bones and injuries and everyone was relieved that he was scraped up but otherwise unhurt.

"Let's get him on the litter and up to his tent. Melchior, maybe there is some medicine you can make to help him?"

"Yes, but I want to look him over when he is back on his own cot. Caspar, then we must speak with him. It's time to find out from him what is really going on and how we can help."

The soldiers climbed easily back up the ravine with the litter between them and soon Balthazar was in his own tent. He was quickly tended to by Illya. He was washed and oiled; a beautiful, fresh garment was put on him and he was lying on priceless linens on his own cot. He looked like the royal magi that he was, but inside he felt broken and confused.

The two other men returned to the tent as Illya was finishing, and at a sign from Melchior, he quickly finished his work and after herding everyone else out of the tent, quietly sat down nearby.

The magi had known each other for a long time and Melchior started, "Balthazar, we are all friends and we want to help you. I can give you a drought that will force you to sleep, but that in itself won't refresh your mind. It's your mind that is ill, isn't it?"

Caspar sat down next to the cot and added, "We want to help you and we can; you are not alone. We just don't know where to start. Help us to help you!"

Balthazar looked at the compassionate faces that were clearly concerned about him and found that he couldn't even speak. He was so sad and anxious, he knew he was sick but it was just beyond him as to what to do. He was helpless and confused. He just wanted to go away.

Melchior placed his hand on Balthazar's forehead, and instantly saw a large vision of the hurt and confusion that raced around in his friend's mind. Melchior also saw the vision that had haunted Balthazar for weeks, he saw Balthazar on one knee in the dirt with a bowed head. He couldn't hear anything but he watched he gazed longingly in front of him, remove his crown, and offer it to someone. Melchior was not new at seeing and interpreting visions, he willed himself to be part of the vision.

It slowly unfolded and he walked into it, he wasn't seen by anyone there as he stepped onto the dirt floor of a stable. Immediately he could smell the fresh straw and clean linens nearby.

There were quiet voices and a small sound coming from the middle of the stable. Melchior's heart leaped, "It is He, Royal Newborn!" Still in the vision, he moved toward the small sounds of the infant and stood quietly when he saw Balthazar kneeling in the dirt in front of a manger, gazing longingly at the newborn.

He could see his posture, one of a supplicant, one that definitely said that the one on his knee was giving his life to the One he would serve. Melchior understood how this picture, without faith and knowledge, would lead Balthazar to believe his kingdom had been conquered and he, as good as dead. But with faith in the Newborn, this vision could only mean life for Balthazar and prosperity for his kingdom.

It was time for Melchior to leave; time was unfolding fast around him. But he hesitated. He wanted so much to just be able to look at the Newborn. He willed himself to stand quietly and then raised his head to the middle of the stable.

He saw the mother as she picked up her infant son and he could see the quiet love in her eyes as she looked down at him in her arms. His father looked to be a strong young man, his smile was easy and he hovered near mother and baby, his rough fingertips softly caressing the newborn's perfect head. There were others around, some were coming out of the nearby inn and groups of shepherds were coming to the stable from out in the fields to simply exclaim quietly and gaze at the child. And Balthazar was kneeling in front of his king.

Then Melchior knelt and lifted his head to look at the infant. His eyes were opened to see the truth of the newborn Son of the Most High God, he saw Perfect God in the form of a baby who left heaven to seek and find his lost people. He saw something else but it was in the future but he knew it was part of what the Son was here to accomplish.

The vision was gone and he ached because it was no more. Aware that he was back in caravan, he remained still while he committed to memory everything he had seen and the truths that he had learned. He again willed himself to move again and looked over at Balthazar on the cot nearby. He quietly chanted ancient prayers for his friend, his soft voice asking for healing and comfort.

He removed two vials from his bag and extracted one leaf from the first container, then tightly replaced the stopper. He took the second vial and removed something that looked like a pea. He placed these two together in his palm and crushed them. He then brought these close to Balthazar's face, saying "Breathe deeply now," he did, "and then once more." He then let the powder fall out of his hand as he continued to speak in a low mesmerizing voice.

"You are asleep now and you will continue to sleep for several hours. You will sleep soundly without concerns and your body will refresh itself immediately. When you awaken, your mind will be clear and you will be hungry."

Balthazar's eyes were closed and his arms were resting quietly at his sides; he didn't know about Melchior's vision and had retreated somewhere in his mind to escape the torment he had endured for weeks. As the two friends walked back to their tents, they discussed Balthazar, "I'm worried, he has a history of anxiety and his father was this way. It is an illness. Most don't realize that his father eventually became mad and was confined for his own safety. The question is can we help our friend and how?"

"Let's rest now Caspar, we will keep a careful eye on him and we will search for and find whatever it takes to heal him. He is as safe as possible now; I know Illya will not let him out of his sight. However, we're both tired, we will start again as the sun is sinking."

Some miles away, another colorful caravan had stopped for the day. The elders were listening to an astonishing young man they had found abandoned in the vast desert.

Week 13

Still Alive

The caravan was a commercial supplier of olive oil. It traveled through the great deserts following the caravan route and had already gone a tremendous distance on this journey. It was a good business and the workers were prosperous, worked together well, and were always traveling. They were on their way now to an out of the way place call Nazareth in order to market their supplies of oil. They were amazed they had discovered a man alone, an outcast, in the desert without supplies and still alive. They had never heard of anyone who survived alone in the desert.

The caravan would have normally left someone an outcast, knowing it was the punishment for only the worst crimes. But this man was different, he wasn't afraid and he wasn't dying! He was simply walking, strongly and surely on the path they were taking. They brought him into the caravan, gave him water, a little food and another cloak and the caravan master sat under his tent to hear his story.

"I thank you for your hospitality and comfort, but you know nothing about me. And I owe you some explanation if I am to accept your kindness."

By this time, several of the elders in the caravan had gathered to listen to Shadrach.

"You know I am an outcast; but what you don't know is the rest of my story. I have served the household of Lord King

Balthazar of Arabia since I was born." At these words all of those in the caravan stopped what they were doing in order to listen. There was a lot of whispering "This one served in the royal household of magi!"

Shadrach continued, "He is a good master, but I have committed a crime against him. In a fight with another of his household, I killed a man. I didn't mean to do it, but it happened. So according to our law, there is only one possible sentence, and that is to be cast out. My lord Balthazar was sad to have to sentence me; I know that.

So you see, you may not want me here in your midst after all. I am a criminal, sentenced to be outcast for the crime of murder. I was and I still am guilty."

Joel looked across at the man, deep into his eyes and said "I have never heard of a true criminal admit his crime. But I do know people, there is always more to the story, did someone provoke you? Did he steal your cattle? But more important than that, how did you survive? No man survives more than one day and a night in the desert, alone."

"You are looking at a guilty man, I was sentenced properly. I confess that freely, but let me tell you how I came to be here instead of dying, as I should have done. The caravan left me behind and my lord Balthazar made sure I had a full skin of water. It doesn't sound like much, but it shows his compassion for me. So I had no reason to think I could live through the night and if I did, I knew I would not survive the coming day. I didn't know what was worse, the guilt I bear, the hellish daytime sun and heat or the freezing cold at night.

First I passed much of the night curled against a mound of sand that was stayed warm for a few hours before the freezing cold numbed my legs and arms. As the day dawned and the sun traveled across the sky, it soon made the desert a white furnace.

The day was long, my water was soon gone and I tried to find shade from the scorching sand that soon burned my skin raw. My stomach started cramping from the lack of water, and so I decided to just wait to die. I fell to the sand and waited for the sun to set. I was hopeless and as I lie there, the sun went down. Immediately I heard movement and I knew my end was near. I thought I had been found by a wild animal that would devour me and finish my existence. Nothing jumped on me so after a while I thought I would face the attack like a man so I raised my head, but instead of looking into the face of a wild beast, I instead saw a golden vision.

I know what you are thinking and you would normally be right. Mirages happen all of the time and this was a typical one; golden light, etc. And I thought the same thing, until the man moved and supported me to sit up and offered me water and finally, food. Most importantly he told me, 'The Messiah will soon be born, sent from God Almighty to save all.' He told me that I am to proclaim him."

Shadrach had quite a crowd around him now, listening intently. "But stranger, you have nothing. You have nothing to proclaim with—no caravan, not a single camel; in fact, you have no water or food. You are almost naked. The desert is perilous; perhaps you didn't see what you thought you saw." All those seated around him were seasoned caravan traders; they knew what they were talking about and nodded their heads in agreement.

Shadrach just shrugged his shoulders. "Then how could I be here? No, he was no mirage and he was no ghost. The messenger told me he was an angel and gave me instructions. He told me to take no provisions; I am to walk. He told me I would meet you; I mean that I would meet a caravan and I was to accept the hospitality of the pilgrims.

That is how and why I am here. I could not have traveled in the desert by myself. You can see me, I am healthy. I am not dying.

And I have already heard about this One the angel proclaims. My lord Balthazar has been called to Him and is following the magnificent star as it leads to Him. I want to tell you about the newborn King of kings who is soon to be born. He has been prophesied and He will be sent from His Father, the Great I Am to save us and establish His kingdom here on earth."

Week 14

Lost

T he elders continued to sit very still in wonder, looking at and listening to Shadrach. They didn't know what to think at first—here was a man who had survived the desert. That was a miracle in itself; and he was telling of the miracle that brought him through the desert, walking, straight to their caravan. They were not learned men in the way that the magi were, but they were smart, successful businessmen and knew when someone was telling the truth and living a miracle.

"We are all Jews here, do you know our laws? We know of the promise of a coming messiah, our prophets proclaim him and we await his arrival to change the world and bring us to Him as He creates His kingdom. We are His chosen people.

We believe you have been chosen to proclaim Him. What would you have us do?

As they spoke Shadrach again felt the presence of the heavenly messenger and knew he was doing exactly what he had been told to do. He started. "He is the Son of the very God that has spoken to us through His prophets. He will soon be born, grow in the Spirit as he matures and will lead us to His kingdom. I am proclaiming Him in order for all Jews to be ready to accept Him and His kingdom.

For myself, I ask that I may travel with you; I will work for you so I will not be a burden. Please allow me to proclaim the Messiah and when I need to leave, I will not take any-thing with me."

~~~~~~~~~~~~~~~~~~~

The caravan was still sleeping. It was about an hour before the time that they usually began to awaken and resume their travel. The sun was still up, though it was below the level of the surrounding hills of sand. The air was cooling quickly from the extreme heat of the day.

Two servants were talking urgently at the opening of one of the beautifully painted tents. The one standing was wringing his hands as the other made a soft sound, stood up quickly, nodded his head and put his hand on the other's shoulder, "Wait here."

Caspar's body servant entered his tent quietly, picking up a pair of slippers in his hand to accompany the light robe he had over his arm. He woke his master, "My lord Caspar," he sounded worried, "Illya, Lord Balthazar's servant is here with very bad news."

Awakening immediately, he asked "News? What? Bring him in."

Illya was immediately there and started crying. "My lord, he is gone! He is gone! I have been at his side all day; he has been still. I went to ensure his fresh water would be delivered soon because I was going to wake him and when I returned, he was gone. He's just gone! I have called and called, I have looked everywhere!" he literally wailed.

Caspar was already up and his body servant was at his side, smoothly helping to guide his arms through the robe. Not taking time to refresh himself, he sent for Melchior and turned back, "You obviously have looked in all of the places that he would go? Our library, private areas?"

Oh yes, I have looked everywhere! Many, many times. He has disappeared! And it will be dark soon." And with that said, everyone in the tent paused, thinking of a sick man alone and possibly lost in the desert.

"Porthos, hand me my cloak. Over his shoulder Caspar continued, "Have you notified Madai?" Illya dumbly nodded and whispered yes; he was standing still, almost in shock. Caspar felt sorry for him but he also knew he didn't have time to wait for Illya to come around, time was the enemy now.

He raised his voice and looked directly at him, "Illya, listen to me. This is what you will do. Give Madai all of the information. All of it about Balthazar, if no one else has and tell him I will be there in moments. We will find him." Illya immediately brought his hands to his face, bowed his head, "Yes majesty, yes. I will ensure he knows everything," and left the tent to send a message to him.

As Caspar hurriedly was dressed, Madai reported to him. "Majesty, is it true? I have already gone to his tent and I see nothing that would lead me to think he has been abducted or anything that will tell us to where he has gone. What do you think?"

"It's too early for me to think. What we do know is this—he is certainly depressed and probably confused, but do we think he intends to harm himself? I don't know. We know that he probably left some hours ago and therefore has been able to go farther than we would have hoped. We know that he has no provisions; Illya said nothing else was disturbed in his tent. So, where did he go?

Melchior's servant announced him as he hurried through the tent's opening. "So he is gone! What do we know about what happened?"

Caspar turned from Madai, "We don't know anything yet but Melchior, I think he has been gone for a while." Melchior nodded in agreement while deep in thought. However, nothing came to him.

Caspar continued, "Illya, I want to see his entire household and be quick." Meanwhile Melchior started to detail the events of the day when most of the caravan were asleep. Turning he stated "I still have to believe that someone has seen him. There is always someone up and about, either security here or even shepherds out with the flocks. Maybe they wouldn't be suspicious of their king being awake and walking about if he were acting like himself, but they definitely would have wondered if he were acting confused or if he was being led away by strangers."

Both men were professionals and immediately asked questions to clarify areas of information that they were unsure of. Together they created a plan, all of the caravan would be enlisted to systematically search their immediate area and then if no clues were found, search in ever-widening circles out in the desert.

Everyone was working from the knowledge that time was slipping away and that they had to be fast. The sun was down now, the caravan had awakened, and the temperature was dropping quickly. With the strong desert wind, the sand was always shifting and tracking someone's footsteps was nearly impossible.

The caravan was notified that lord Balthazar was ill and missing, maybe he wandered in delirium. The cattle were kept in their pens, watered and fed; then the search was on. All three households were looking through tents and supplies; anywhere someone could possibly be if they were injured, confused, or trying to hide.

Word returned that he was not found inside the caravan and it appeared that he had taken nothing with him.

Caspar and Melchior were together at Balthazar's household in order to maintain the search, "Are we absolutely sure that he left on his own free will? He wasn't abducted?"

"I don't believe anyone else came into the area and took him. I just don't know about his health and most importantly, the health of his mind. He was depressed, no he IS depressed and agonizing over many things, past and present. So we must believe he has set off on his own, to do something we just don't understand."

"We must get to him soon."

~~~~~~~~~~~~~~~~~~~~

Back at Balthazar's palace, in their bedroom, his wife, Deborah, was having a dream. She was asleep and turned over to find her husband gone from the bed, the linen was still warm where he had been. She sat up and thought she saw him on the balcony. Arising, she followed only to not find him nearby but in the garden a few steps below her. She could still see him and called out, but he didn't seem to hear. He stopped at one of the many fountains and seemed to be listening to someone. She decided to go to him and as she came to the far end of the gardens, she saw a small boy there. He was dressed as a shepherd and had a staff. He looked as though he was waiting for her, "Shepherd, I thought I saw my husband nearby. Have you seen him?

He answered, "No, my lady, but I am blind and cannot see. But I do know my lord Balthazar has called for you but right now he is entertaining a visitor. I can hear them clearly; can I take you to him?"

The dream ended and Deborah awoke quickly. She had been around prophets and seers all of her life. She dwelled with those who searched for signs from heaven and she knew she had been given a message. She would be criticized but Balthazar needed her and she was going to find her husband; she would notify her household, and set out today.

Week 15

The Search

⚜

Melchior and Caspar personally took charge of the ever-widening search. They had divided the area surrounding the caravan into sectors and then identified the vectors moving away from the household by yards and miles. Their staff was interviewing everyone in the caravan, not just asking if they had seen Balthazar, but if they had seen anyone else, stranger or not, acting suspiciously. Had they heard anything, or was there anything at all they could contribute?

Balthazar's household had been in service to him and his family for many years, most of them had been born within the household and all were truly loyal to him. His household had already made sure he wasn't injured and lying somewhere in the caravan itself, now they were fanning out in their part of the search and you could already hear their voices calling.

Meanwhile, Caspar and a large group were searching another sector of the immediate desert. They had surveyed the map of the area and knew they were close to a heavily traveled caravan route. They could have picked up a wandering and confused man, so messengers were riding out to intercept caravans within an established radius. Caspar didn't think a very large radius was required, Balthazar had gone out in the daytime and no one would have been able to travel very far on foot and there were no camels missing. If he was out in the desert, he wouldn't survive long on foot, and of course there were bandits and foraging animals.

The first search of the campsite and surrounding area yielded nothing. They found only that there was nothing taken from Balthazar's tent, no food or water was gone, and nothing was found that looked like a struggle had taken place. His servant was entirely trustworthy and was distraught. Illya reported that nothing in the tent was removed, the bed linens were neatly drawn back and even his sandals were in order, at the foot of the bed.

As the night wore on, the activity continued even as the wind made the desert biting cold.

Caspar returned to the large tent to confer once again with Melchior. "Have you seen the star? It isn't moving. It still blazes in the west but it is waiting."

"I noticed it! It has suspended its journey and I hope that means it waits for Balthazar."

"I have nothing new to report. Any news?"

Melchior stood to pace. "No one saw or heard anything out of the ordinary. But perhaps that is the answer, there wasn't anything unusual; maybe the key is finding out what happened that looked so ordinary that anyone who saw it would not even think about it later."

"Are you saying that instead of looking for something violent, we should be looking for clues from daily activities?"

"I don't know, but you and I both know that Balthazar was seriously anxious and depressed. We know that the mixture of medicine and suggestion that I gave him didn't calm him enough to allow him to sleep long. He was up very soon after we left him, I believe he stayed on his cot and became more and more disoriented. That is why Illya was caught off guard. No one could have normally expected him to be awake or doing anything for hours.

The moon has crossed the sky and soon the new day will begin. If we don't find him soon, we will have to separate and take shifts during the day."

"And what of our star?"

"I think we both know; we will stay here, looking for our friend."

"Agreed."

As the magi were talking, the sun was lighting up the sky on the other side of the hill and the day was almost there.

The meticulous search was continuing when Madai was approached by a soldier with news and he immediately issued an order that sent the man back toward the desert.

He then turned to walk toward the magi's tent. He looked at Illya, and Illya nodded to him and bowed and leaned over to speak to Melchior. "My lord, the shepherd boy is not with the flock. He cannot be found."

Finally information! Both magi paused as Madai continued. "I am finding out when he was last seen. It may be as far back as yesterday, he stays with the sheep all of the time and takes meals out with them. We got the report that several of his sheep wandered over to where the water is kept and that is unusual.

When they were herded back to where the boy stays, he was not found. His staff is gone, but all of the sheep are accounted for so we don't believe he is searching for a lost lamb."

~~~~~~~~~~~~~~~~~~~~~

"But you, Bethlehem Ephrathah,
though you are little among the clans of Judah,
Yet out of you will come for me the One who will be
Ruler in Israel

Micah 5:2

Shadrach startled awake from a troubled sleep. He had not been troubled since he had decided to follow the Newborn and proclaim Him. He was instantly aware that there was a problem somewhere and he rolled from his blanket to his knees to pray about this problem.

"Where do I fit in? And what should I do", he asked.

He knew immediately so he got up and started toward the front of the tent. The group would continue on their way soon, to another small place in an out of the way place of the world, Bethlehem.

"Bethlehem, what a tiny place for the entire world to be gathering!"

~~~~~~~~~~~~~~~~~~~~

Deborah had used all of her forcefulness to gather the household leaders and make arrangements to leave as quickly as possible. "I'm leaving to follow after my husband, I have been told in a dream that he needs me. So I will do as I am bid."

She pushed through their questions and anxieties. What she didn't mention to most of the advisors and officials was that she understood clearly the danger that Balthazar was facing. She had secretly nursed him through many of these types of attacks; they were anxieties that accumulated in his mind until he couldn't function anymore. She had learned the art of healing and calming his mind from Melchior and because she was so helpful, no one was aware about his problem.

What she didn't know at this point was how far he had sunk in his confusion and fear. She had to be there as soon as possible. She had sent word to Melchior and Caspar telling them of her plans.

One official protested, "My lady, do you know what has happened to our lord Balthazar and where he is? You must know we could send messengers and wait for word to return back to us. Then you could send others to him. Otherwise, there are still so many questions."

Deborah rounded on him, "Caipha, don't misunderstand. I'm not the child that I used to be and I'm telling you to complete the duties I gave you. I am leaving on this journey and the kingdom is in exceptionally good hands. I have created no danger for us; but, I know that I have a place in these events. I will go."

Week 16

The Shepherd and Balthazar

$\mathscr{D}$

Deborah swiftly walked to their daughter's rooms in the palace after sending word to her sons requesting they attend her as soon as possible. It was still early so she was expecting to find her asleep with her maid somewhere nearby, so she was amazed to see her daughter, awake and pacing.

Both women turned to her when she entered the room and after the maid bowed her head and started a small curtsy, Hasa held out her hands to her mother, saying "I had the same dream. I am praying for him, now. You must go, but I will follow you in dreams and pray for your success. Who are you taking with you?"

Deborah was not overly surprised that Hasa had the dream, she was gifted and her knowledge of the gift was growing very strong. "Your brother, Jabael, will come with me. I want him along if we need to negotiate politically, that is his strength. But I worry about you. You know your father thinks of you continually and would never want anything to happen to you, especially if it were because he or I weren't here. You are truly the daughter of our heart.

They were sitting on a silk-covered divan that was near a small heated urn that gave off just enough warmth to keep the desert nights comfortable, they both turned to look out the large windows at the sun as it touched the top of the nearby hill. Deborah could now see her daughter's face in the growing sunlight, and knew it was all right for her to go. Hasa was no longer the child that both parents often acted like she was.

~~~~~~~~~~~~~~~~~~~~

At the same time, Caspar and the search parties had all returned to the caravan site. They had searched within the circumferences they had hoped they would find Balthazar. They now started to think that Balthazar and perhaps the shepherd boy had been attacked by wild animals and eaten or even carried away to be sold as slaves by bandits that were known to sweep the desert. If they had been attacked by bandits, however; they knew there would be ransom messages.

However, there was hope. There were no tracks; absolutely nothing to follow so maybe, just maybe something else had happened.

Melchior and Caspar listened as Madai reported, "If he had been attacked by animals, there would have been blood and there is none. If he had been captured, we would have heard about it, it's obvious who he is and that we have money to bargain with. And we haven't even seen another messenger."

Melchior then said, "So, what has happened to him? Since he can't just disappear, we have to think now about the possibility that he doesn't want to be found."

"Of course he does. Why do you say this thing?"

Melchior leaned forward, "No, you don't understand my meaning. It shows how very ill Balthazar is. In most circumstances, this wouldn't have happened, but he isn't in his right mind and he is very anxious. We don't know what he may have been thinking and what he might actually do.

We need to start thinking about locating a man who doesn't want to be found. We need to change our strategy. We need to find him soon; it may already be too late."

Illya approached with news, "Majesties, a rider from my lord Balthazar's household has arrived."

"Please, bring him here."

A servant of the household appeared quickly, all business—he bowed, "Majesties, I have come with a note and I have ridden ahead of 20 riders who will assist in looking for Lord Balthazar."

Everyone in the tent was quiet, looking at the rider. Caspar demanded, "You've just ridden here from his palace? On who's orders and how do you know Lord Balthazar needs to be found?" He immediately wondered if Balthazar's disappearance was something more; perhaps treason starting at the palace?

"And what else do you know?" started Madai, approaching the rider menacingly. Everyone was tired and worried, and tempers were thin.

Melchior held up his hand, "No, wait." He had been looking carefully at the rider, at his sandy clothes and at his drawn, pale face. The young man looked very tired; Melchior became quiet. He could feel the concern for Balthazar and more than that, he could clearly see the man was loyal to his household's master. He was not part of any deception.

Melchior made a sign for him to continue. "Please lords, my master's wife personally bade me ride as quickly as possible. She has had a dream; I have her message that will tell you everything."

Opening a sandy, worn carrier, the rider removed a beautiful scroll that was obviously bound by the seal of the palace of King Balthazar and presented it to the magi.

Caspar accepted the scroll and he inspected the seal closely as he turned back to his desk. Melchior remained seated. Suddenly smiling, he already knew what the message would say. "It's from Deborah! She is on her way now."

Caspar looked up at him, no longer surprised at his abilities. He read out loud the rest of the message, "Both she and their daughter, Princess Hasa, have been visited by a dream that told them about Balthazar and she is traveling here."

"Remember, Deborah's father and mother were both great seers and prophets and we know their daughter has great powers of her own. Amazing powers, indeed. So, Deborah is on her way! "

"However, she must arrive soon in order to find him alive. How long do you think it will take her to arrange a caravan," asked Caspar."

The rider was listening to the conversation and added "Forgive me lords; she is on her way, just hours behind me."

~~~~~~~~~~~~~~~~~~~~~

Balthazar's head pounded so hard that he could hear it. When he tried to open his eyes, they didn't work. He couldn't stay awake any longer, he tried to call out for help but only a whimper came from his lips. He could remember that he had walked out of his tent, he was determined to reason through his anxieties and thought he would find the answers if he could just walk.

He realized soon that he really shouldn't be out walking after being given the strong medication along with the hypnotic suggestion by Melchior. Not only was he dizzy and sick to his stomach but he also couldn't make out where he was going.

He had wrapped an old cloak around him as he ducked out of his tent so no one would recognize him because he just wanted to quietly walk by himself. He walked until he was very, very tired and looked up in surprise that he couldn't see the back of the caravan any longer.

He raised his hand to his eyes to look into the distance and he stumbled at a small hill in the sand. He slowly rose only to get dizzy again and fall down the rest of the sand dune. This one happened to be very big, and his slide finally stopped when he hit his head on a group of rocks that jutted out of the hillside.

Coming to a stop, his head looked like it had been sliced by a sword, his blood flowed freely and he felt himself drift away and hover above his still body.

~~~~~~~~~~~~~~~~~~~~~

Deborah felt a cold wall slam into her body. She knew this as one of the signs that foretold a serious illness or injury and pending death, so she steeled herself. She had come to believe in the Newborn whose star her husband followed in order to worship him. And as she had come to know the Newborn and His destiny, she trusted in Him. She immediately held up her hands to pray for the one or ones who were in mortal danger; she didn't know for whom she prayed but she was compelled to pray with all of her soul.

As she prayed, she was startled to hear her own voice calling out for help from the Newborn King. She had never uttered His name before and she found that she knew Him and His power. She petitioned Him as someone who had the absolute right to ask the King of kings for anything. Very soon, she felt power as she had never known it before being released through her prayers and her faith. This power of goodness and mercy seemed to flow like water over a dam and she was changed.

Week 17

Shepherd

D ebra took another deep breath and straightened her shoulders as she felt the power that had been released. She urged the camels on as their smaller household and protecting soldiers continued to follow the original caravan's path into the desert.

She had left the next to the eldest son in charge of the household and to administer the court while they were gone. She knew he was a good administrator and would easily take care of all of the duties that were necessary.

She had brought their oldest son with her, to act in his father's behalf and transact any necessary business during Balthazar's recuperation. The two middle sons had been contacted by messenger to tell them of their mother's journey, but they were already in positions of authority for the kingdom and she didn't want them to leave their respective courts in such a quick manner. They would be able to help if needed.

She and Balthazar studied prophecies and the heavens; they had both become aware of the One who was to be born that would establish His kingdom on earth. They had talked about Him as they studied and they believed their lands could have a part in his mighty, eternal kingdom. She didn't ever think Arabia would be conquered by this Newborn King, she thought he was more; but Balthazar was concerned about what this all could mean for not only the kingdom, but for both of them.

The heavens and prophets had talked about Him for almost 1,000 years and together, they would see Him come into His own kingdom. What a time to be alive!

Right now Debra knew what she was called to do; she was to help bring Balthazar safely out of this situation so he could greet and worship the Newborn. Otherwise, how could their household be counted and recognized as supporters of this new King and His kingdom?

~~~~~~~~~~~~~~~~~~~~

In the common tent in the caravan, Melchior and Caspar looked up at the heavens, the beautiful star was there; and it was still.

"It waits for us. It waits for Balthazar."

"But Caspar, try as I might, I cannot find any signs of where he may be or how he got away from the caravan. I am fearful for him."

Caspar raised his head and while avoiding looking at Melchior and at Illya standing nearby, said "We must find him soon; I too am losing hope of finding him alive."

"And, of course, what can we tell Deborah?"

The members of the households that were in the caravan continued their jobs even though they were no longer traveling. There was always work to do; some mended tents and coverings, and others kept the flocks and food, still others ensured all were safe from the constant threat of robbers.

~~~~~~~~~~~~~~~~~~~~

Well away from the caravan, the shepherd boy sat very still, he was blind but had developed strong senses to help him with the sheep. Now he knew they were frightened and were pushing toward him to get away from something.

If there was a wild animal pursuing them, he would have heard it and he had been successful recently when he had to actually fight a predator. But now, he heard nothing so he was waiting. He knew the caravan was unmoving and lying at the edge of the crop of trees just over the hill. So he followed the sheep to an area they had found where they were he could hear they were all milling around.

As he walked up a small rise, he found some rocks to climb up on. He would call the sheep to him from there and find out what was happening. He approached the rocks and the sheep that were following him scattered. And now he knew why. He could hear a faint noise from something wounded and he could smell blood.

"There must be a wounded animal that has taken refuge in the rocks", he thought. As he stopped his climb up the hill, he listened to find out exactly where the animal was hiding. He heard nothing else at first, then heard a faint breathing— no movement.

Yes, he could definitely smell blood and that was what was scaring the sheep. They were skittish, but he noticed they didn't run away. He had first thought this could be one of his flock; but now he knew it wasn't; he knew the sounds of his own, and this one was different.

He stood very still and lifted his face to the wind that swirled around him, listening with all that was within him. This was a human! He was sure!

He softly called out, "Hello. Are you hurt?"

He was immediately answered with a low groan that ended in a weak cough. He turned toward the sound and raised his rod, intending to be ready to strike if this was a robber or outcast that was threatening. Then he didn't hear the sounds again.

He moved aside a lamb that had stopped in his path, then called softly again, "Hello, do you need help?" No answer and no sound returned.

The shepherd paused for a long minute. He then started toward the spot where he had last heard the groan; now holding the lamb that seemed so anxious in his left arm and keeping his rod held high in his right hand, ready to strike.

He felt the lamb shiver under his arm as he stepped onto something sticky in the sand. He knew that someone very ill or injured was right there and they strangely didn't want to be found.

A leper? No, there were no colonies nearby that he knew of.

He called again, "Hello? Let me help you," and then heard a plea in response, "Here."

The shepherd boy quietly comforted the small lamb under his arm and turned toward the voice. He didn't think of any danger now, he acted quickly just as he did when any one of his lambs were in peril, taking quick steady steps, listening carefully, and ready to act to defend the defenseless.

He found an area in the sand that felt as though it had been dug away, perhaps when a body had fell over it, and then he came to some limestone that indicated the edge of the hill. Following the path in the sand, his hand found a stream of sticky, copper-smelling blood, and then finally, some sand that seemed to move at his touch. He had found a person, still alive.

Week 18

Found

W as this a trick? And if it was, who could it be? He had accounted for all of his sheep and they were all well, so the blood was not theirs and this wasn't a poacher. The boy bent down, carefully arranging the small lamb that clung to him as he felt in the sand for the injured man, but who could it be?

His hand found the shoulder of a man, and at almost the same time he realized who this was. Lord Balthazar! But something was very wrong with him. This was a royal mage, a king who ruled an entire country and he was on a pilgrimage to welcome a newborn king, as befitting royal households. Why was he here?

"My Lord Balthazar? Is this you? Are you hurt?"

The form lying in the sand moved slightly and seemed to try to speak.

The blind shepherd knelt at the injured man, and prepared to do what he did exceptionally well: console the injured, locate the wounds and then bind them so he could get further help. He had done this for his lambs for as long as he could remember. His hand came upon the trails of blood that still oozed from the great wounds at Balthazar's head, he followed it to where patches of his head and scalp had been sliced away and they hung by mere strings of skin.

The injured Balthazar moaned more loudly and was still. The boy acted quickly and reached into the bag that was slung on his back and found the skin of water and the strips of clean cloths he carried to tend to the sheep that sometimes were injured.

"My lord, please have some water," there was no response and he knew the man was close to death, he seemed to be surrounded by a pool of his own blood. The shepherd poured water onto the cloths and bound them about Balthazar's head and neck. They absorbed the blood and he hoped that would help stop or at least slow down the flow. He knew he couldn't move him nor could he leave him to go get help.

But he couldn't let Balthazar die, "Oh what has happened and why are you he out here?" he thought.

The boy had always lived among the sheep, alone. He didn't remember if he ever had a family except for those in Balthazar's household, he certainly didn't remember a mother or a father. He was cared for as part of those who served the royal family. Even after the accident and he became blind, he knew that he had to continue to care for the flocks, what else would he do and then what would happen to him?"

Though he was the smallest among the workers in the household, the difficult times in his life had made the shepherd boy strong and self reliant. He knew how to care for the ones who were defenseless and in need, because that is a shepherd's life.

He reached to check the arms and legs of the man to find if he was further injured, he could tell he had fallen from the top of the hill and had hit the rocks with his head. He was thankful that he found no obvious broken bones. As he checked the man for further injuries, he hummed the songs and tunes he always sung to calm his sheep. The flock gathered around them, even though they were frightened by the over powering smell of blood, they knew their shepherd.

The boy was still working when all at once, the flock scattered and at the same time, he heard the low growls and breathing of predators that had found the source of the smell of blood. The shepherd didn't think, he got up to his feet, and standing over the body of Balthazar, he turned in the direction of what sounded to be a pack of wild animals.

The packs were the most dangerous to fight because they were wild beasts that hunted together and were known to take down almost every animal they encountered.

His loud shouts and hisses usually scared off single animals that preyed on the flock; but it wouldn't work with a pack. This time, the animals just paused long enough to see that there was just one of him, alone, and realize that there were many of them.

They were perfect predators and they all turned to him. They saw a perfect target and a perfect opportunity.

They excitedly approached, sniffing and whining at the smell of the blood and the sight of the injured man on the ground. The flock had long scattered but the pack wasn't interested in them any longer.

The boy didn't back down, he squared his feet and brought his rod out in front of them in order to strike the first animal that got in range. He knew it was futile and that the fight wouldn't last long; the pack had encircled them and was closing in fast.

A mighty shout seemed to split the air at the same time well-aimed rocks pelted the circling pack. The beasts stopped and turned to the attackers, snarling. They were mad but they moved away from the shepherd slowly and stood uncertainly as they assessed the approaching challenge. Then with frustrated barks, they turned quickly and fled.

The captain of the guards that had driven away the pack ordered his men to go forward quickly to help the two at the bottom of the hill. They were part of a caravan headed west and were out scouting for a caravan some miles behind them when they saw the boy and the injured man. They watched them until they thought they understood the situation and ensured their caravan was not in danger.

The captain sent a scout back to tell his commander of their encounter, he knew he would be told to do what he could to help the older, injured man and his small protector. As he approached the two he could tell the man on the ground had been seriously injured and that the small protector was a shepherd boy, who seemed to be blind! The soldiers were helping get the flocks back to the shepherd and then would return to their duties.

He asked, "Shepherd, what has happened to this man? And how did a small thing like yourself think you were going to save both of you? Why, you are blind!"

"Sire, our caravan is over that hill, he said pointing to the east, "thank you for saving us. I am the flock's shepherd and I safeguard them. Please help us; I have come upon my master and he has been hurt. I cannot leave him to go to get help from the caravan and I fear for him."

The captain had casually taken a seat as he talked to the boy and he glanced over on the ground and then pointed asking, "Who is he?"

"He is King Balthazar, of Arabia, Royal Magi and my master. We are on a pilgrimage and I don't know what evil thing has happened to him but I do know the caravan must be searching for him and he needs help."

The guard had startled up from his seat and almost slid to a stop at the boy's side. He had never seen a mage before and he didn't know how he would recognize one. The shepherd stood his ground next to his master.

Then the guard let out a deep breath, because not only did he finally see that the fabrics of the man's gown were priceless but he saw Balthazar's arm. The man muttered, "Pardon me, your majesty", as he slowly moved away the sleeve from the full insignia tattooed on the injured man. He stopped when he clearly saw the emblem that was given to Balthazar at his royal birth and the surrounding crest of the magi. This could only mean that this injured man was truly King Balthazar, Royal Magi.

A king! And mage! He had only heard of magi and their powers. He knew they existed and that they knew more about everything than normal people. They searched for truth and because of their studies and their knowledge, they were often able to heal sicknesses, see into the future from searching the heavens, and it had even been said they could talk to and see spirits.

So, what was one of these men doing out here? This changed everything; he stood and bowed to the still form of Balthazar. He then looked again measuringly at the shepherd boy, and then signaled one of his scouts, and everyone seemed to move quickly at once.

"Well, young one. He could not have a better protector. At first, I thought you had attacked your master and had brought him out here to kill him but we saw your bravery in standing against that wild pack. We have seen you since we crested the hill, but we needed to get pretty close in order to scare off the pack so they wouldn't decide they had enough time to snatch either one of you before they ran away."

A soldier appeared, "Captain, our prince will be here soon; he wants to see the man."

Without taking his eyes off of the boy, he responded, "Shepherd, we will await our master, Prince Nessar of Egypt."

Week 19

Prince Nessar

A fter announcing they would wait for the prince, the captain of the guard set about directing several of his men to gather up Lord Balthazar onto a stretcher that they quickly made of linens between staffs they carried. The shepherd boy stayed close to his master and hoped he would awaken. He was also anxious to get word to his caravan.

The captain asked, "We have a surgeon who has been summoned to attend his Majesty and one of my riders has sighted a caravan over the next hill. Would that be where you belong?"

Before the boy could answer, the captain turned and there was a lot of bustling and talking that seemed to signal that the prince was approaching. The captain kneeled briefly and then waited for him to speak and when he did, his voice was quiet and full of authority.

"Captain, who have you found?"

"Your majesty, we are told the injured man is King Balthazar. And I myself have seen the royal crest on his arm." The shepherd boy listened to the captain describe what they had observed and what had been done. He could tell from his manner that the he considered the prince to be more than just their master, but one who was just and thoughtful. Each man's voice conveyed the respect they felt as men doing a hard job for a man who deserved their best. This gave the shepherd boy courage to speak.

"Master, if I may speak?"

It became very quiet. The prince looked down at the very small boy. He saw the obvious injuries and understood that he was blind but that he still worked hard for the household. He had been told that this young shepherd had courageously stood to fight for his king when he was seriously injured. The prince considered the boy had done a man's job and had done it well.

"Well, he does speak! So, mighty warrior, what do you have to say?"

"Your highness, I am but a lowly shepherd, but this is my master, Lord Balthazar, Royal Mage, King of Arabia. We are traveling on a pilgrimage and he has been injured. He has somehow gotten away from the caravan and everyone must be desperate to find him. Other magi are traveling in the caravan and await word of him."

As they spoke, the prince's own surgeon had arrived and was looking at Balthazar, pouring oils on his wound and binding his head. He offered him water and then reported that he, for some reason, still appeared to be sleeping.

Still talking and curious, the prince had questions for the boy, "Other magi? Who are these? And are they all in a pilgrimage? To where?"

The boy forgot his fear and said, "There are three royal magi: my master; Lord Caspar, Maharaja of the regions of India; and, His Majesty, King Melchior of Persia. They study the stars and ancient prophecies and know a mighty king is to soon be born and they are traveling to honor him.

"How do they know this pending birth? I am unaware and my kingdom is closer to this area than theirs. I would have received the summons also."

"It is not a summons that they received. It is the star."

The prince was intrigued to learn more about the magi. He knew their kingdoms and realized their pilgrimage was leading them close to where his caravan now waited. He had seen the magnificent light in the sky and he agreed that it seemed to wait now but he didn't know what it meant. He knew the magi would have answers and he longed to speak to them, and; of course, to help in any way he could.

Prince Nessar was the Egyptian Royal Prince and he knew that one day he would rule his country so he wanted good friends who would be powerful allies. Royal Magi were the ultimate in power, they ruled powerful sovereign nations that had not bowed to any invading forces and they had studied and learned natural phenomenon so they could read nature and the heavens. The prince eagerly continued his questions, "That great shining light that has been traveling in the sky for months? It is a star and it speaks to them?"

"It guides them, it doesn't speak. But the King will soon be born; my master says he has seen the angels that proclaimed this mighty one. And I was healed."

The prince looked carefully at the shepherd boy, he believed everything that he had told him and was surprised at the last thing the boy mentioned. The shepherd certainly didn't look like he had been healed. His face and head wounds were very much in evidence. How odd.

The small boy had lowered himself to sit in a tiny little space at the foot of his master's cot, still guarding him. The prince ordered food and water brought to the boy and that he be given a place by his master to keep watch over him.

The prince thought again of magi, of those who were educated and watched the heavens and explored old scrolls for news of the One who was to be born and he was in awe of them. They were revered and some regions even worshipped them; and they were traveling to greet and honor this royal newborn King.

He made up his mind; he didn't want to be left out! He would deliver this mage and his servant back to them and he would be able to ask questions of those who had answers about the Newborn.

This King, who the very heavens and its angels proclaim! The prince had seen this giant light that traveled slowly through the heavens at night and was even visible during the day, but it had never occurred to anyone he knew that it should be followed. He felt a strong connection to the star's message and wondered where it would lead.

Meanwhile, the prince's caravan had sent out an envoy to the larger caravan behind them to take the message that King Balthazar had been found and to emphasize he was very weak. The magi were welcomed to the prince's caravan and he could be transferred from there whenever they thought it was safe for him to be moved further.

Week 20

Good News

❦

"**M**y lords, a messenger has ridden into camp, from a nearby Egyptian caravan that includes their master, Prince Nessar."

"A rider! Perhaps this is good news." Melchior had been updating their search maps and called through the opening in the tent to Caspar. "There is news! I think we need some good news now."

Caspar and Melchior both were seated to receive the messenger. He was escorted into the tent; he didn't look as though he had ridden far, and their thoughts were confirmed when he spoke.

"Your majesties, thank you for the honor of your presence. I carry greetings and a message from my master, His Royal Highness, Prince Nessar, Crown Prince of Egypt. 'We have found the injured King Balthazar, he is seriously hurt. He is being attended by our surgeons, but they would welcome your expertise.'

The elder, King Melchior, inclined his head, "Please convey our greetings to Prince Nessar, and our sincere appreciation for caring for our colleague. We offer our hospitality to you and we gratefully accept your prince's invitation." Inside Melchior and Caspar were jumping up and down, cheering and impatient to get to Balthazar's side. But royal protocol was important and a messenger from Crown Prince Nessar needed to be treated well.

The rider bowed, but he could not help to continue to stare in amazement at the magi. They were the source of legends. The men themselves, they had obviously been traveling for a while, and they sat surrounded by amazing instruments. Some of them, it was said, could magically see up into the heavens and speak to the stars. There were dozens of colorful, bubbling flasks of teas and other liquids, and stacks and stacks of rolled scrolls that he knew contained ancient secrets.

He knew they were royalty that studied the heavens and searched for truth and knowledge, they knew all languages and could see into the future and often read minds. It was said they knew magic that could turn plain rocks into precious jewels and gold; and they could turn their enemies or just stupid people into animals. He made a quick note to look around closely at the animals outside; maybe he knew one of them!

The messenger was still staring at everything in the tent and jumped when Caspar bounded out of his chair after he received the news. He grabbed Melchior by the arm, "He has been found! Let's go to him."

The rider bowed yet again as he was led out of the tent by one of Melchior's attendants. Illya had chosen several guards to accompany him to the other caravan with the messenger and he was impatient to be there as quickly as possible. The other magi would follow as soon as they gathered the necessary supplies and secured a tribute for the prince who had rescued Balthazar.

Unknown to them all, Queen Deborah, Balthazar's wife, was approaching quickly from the east in a smaller, quickly-moving caravan and had discovered the prince's caravan some miles in front of hers. They sent a messenger ahead; even so, she could barely stop herself from just racing on. One didn't just ride into the camps of travelers in the vast desert. That was foolish. There were too many bandits and armies of mercenaries scouring these areas for foolhardy travelers, so one had to constantly be on guard.

Her son moved his camel closer to hers. She smiled to herself, he knew she could be impetuous and he was afraid she just may ride off to the caravan ahead of all of the others. She took another deep breath, "Control yourself!" she sternly thought. She had ridden for days now with very little rest but she was strong and eager to find Balthazar.

She didn't know how strongly his anxiety and depression had claimed him. She was worried because she usually took care of him in his private rooms in the palace, away from others and prying eyes. Deborah and Balthazar kept his condition a secret because it would be seen as a weakness by enemies.

He had always had a personality that demanded perfection from himself. When he had inherited his crown he matured to the point that he worked hard to be wise enough to govern his kingdom well, he truly wanted to establish a good royal government. But he often lost faith in himself and then his anxieties would grow. She was hoping she was not too late to help him now.

Riders could be heard returning and Deborah turned to squeeze her son's hand. He turned to the rider anxiously and said "Is there news of my father, is the next caravan his?"

"Sire, the caravan just beyond the hill belongs to the Egyptian royal household of Prince Nessar, he welcomes you. Your father, our lord, is being cared for in their midst as we speak! Lord Balthazar was found collapsed, after he had been wandering in the desert! He is very ill. His servant, Illya is with him and I left soldiers there also."

"So we're not too late! Onward, get fresh animals for us, we will ride with a small force ahead to the caravan."

Deborah leaned forward, "I am ready! Please, quickly, Merriam bring my chests of medicines."

"Mother, please, we must be able to represent the kingdom well. You know what father would say. Take a minute to change into less dusty clothes and have Merriam arrange your hair.

"Merriam, please take my mother aside to dress her, no matter how she may protest!"

"Son! We must hurry at all costs we must go to him quickly."

"We are almost there, and when the fresh animals are saddled, we will be ready also. Will you ride into the camp, wild-eyed and dusty, presenting yourself as the Queen of Lord Balthazar, King of Arabia? We have gifts to take and remember, Illya is with him."

Turning aside to his aide, Jabael dropped his voice, "The question is why was my father out in the desert? And now he has been rescued by another caravan with only Illya in attendance? What has happened to the household caravan?"

They continued quietly discussing these ideas as Deborah was dressed. "What are the chances there has been an attack or a revolt in the caravan household? Illya is there and he is absolutely trustworthy. What has happened? We will get to the bottom of this."

Illya had arrived just minutes before Deborah's outriders had approached the camp. He had brought linens and many of the medicines that both he and then Melchior may need for Balthazar. He wept when he saw his master, whispering, "My lord, we have all been so worried. I have been asking the Newborn to guide you."

Balthazar was not moving and he didn't respond. He didn't know how he had been found, but was listening to what the other servants and Illya were saying as he was cleaned of the sand and blood that covered him from head to toe.

". . .the shepherd boy found his master and guarded him from wild beasts, saving his life!"

"But how? Did you know the boy is blind? How could he save the king?"

"I don't know, but it's true. Maybe he wove a magic spell?"

"No silly, shepherds don't have magic. Magi have magic." And as that last sentence seemed to hang in the air, Prince Nessar's household all paused to look at Balthazar in wonder.

Meanwhile, Prince Nessar was also amazed. Never in his life had he seen so much going on in such a short time in the big dusty desert! He had traveled caravan routes many times and had found the desert isolated and completely silent. Not now—he had found a mysterious and priestly mage that the whole world seemed to know and respect for his knowledge of the ancient world and the worlds to come.

Magi were almost holy and were the stuff of legends. Not only had his caravan had rescued one, but he was being guarded by a small, thin and, don't forget, blind shepherd boy, in the middle of the desert. Now, he would have the opportunity to entertain other magi who had been traveling with their friend, and a rider had just returned to say King Balthazar's wife was approaching in another caravan and had sent greetings, requesting to enter his camp!

The prince entertained continually and royally, of course, when he was at his palace but he had never received visitors, especially royal ones, while traveling.

"Her Majesty, Queen Deborah, wife of King Balthazar of Arabia and her son, Crown Prince El-Jabael request the privilege of entering your presence."

Prince Nessar immediately rose to greet the two, he believed they would want to hurry to the bedside of King Balthazar but he was no longer sure. He inclined his head as the tall slim figures quickly came into the large receiving tent and as he rose and went forward to greet them, his breath caught.

Week 21

Queen Deborah

Q ueen Deborah didn't follow the custom of covering herself in voluminous black robes; she was royally attired as befitting her station and was wearing layers of airy fabrics that were the colors of early morning. Her head was uncovered and a petite diadem was evident. Her intelligent eyes showed concern.

Unlike many other royal families of the time, Deborah was queen in every sense of the word. She was not a consort; she had royal powers and ran her court independently. She and Balthazar had both been born royal heirs and they both had been educated for a sovereign's job. Deborah often attended to business affairs and their financing; her steadiness when responding to requests and needs had contributed vastly to Arabia's strength and security. So she came to this meeting with Prince Nessar fully knowing how to act and how to respond, if necessary.

Her son was sturdy and tall, protective while standing slightly behind at the left of the strong queen. The rest of the attending party bowed to the prince as the queen and her son walked to him. She stopped just in front of him as he did her the honor of bowing; she seemed delighted, "Prince Nessar, thank you for your hospitality. We are honored more than you can know. We have many fond memories of our countries' long friendship and we wish to send greetings to your sovereign parents."

"My lady, I assure you that our kingdom will always be the best of friends and allies with yours. My father and mother will be overjoyed that you remember them and would want me to offer you any assistance and acts of friendship before you can even request them." Nessar bowed deeply this time and continued, "Please command me."

Nessar looked up at the queen. What captured the prince's attention was that she appeared so very fragile, as though she had no strong bonds to this earth, and was dressed in colors from hazy blues to airy mauves. Her eyes exactly matched the outer lawyer of her gown, they were softly shaded sky blue and he was lost. She was obviously use to his type of scrutiny and even though she looked as though she was wanted to speak, she was still and gazed back at him boldly.

And she was escorted by two angels! He had never seen real ones but he had admired paintings of angels and knew these were what were standing right in front of him! They weren't just standing quietly and still, they paced in the tent and were obviously looking around. The two looked like they were on guard and unfortunately didn't have a pleasant angelic look on either of their faces.

The one who kept closest to the queen was wearing a long gown like the ones worn by most desert travelers. His hood was slung back to reveal a mostly hairless head and a face that looked like he was listening to everyone's thoughts. He was of average height, his arms were bare and he had a leather guard on his bow arm that extended to his wrist and something that looked like a crossbow on his shoulder. He also had a pair of short swords in his belt. Nessar watched him look around once again and then walk back to the queen and then turn and fix his eyes on him. Nessar wisely didn't move.

The other angel was tall, had longer dark hair that was pulled back at his neck and was wearing the usual desert clothing but had a vest on over the gown. Unlike the other, he looked like a soldier who had seen plenty of battles. He had a long sword over his back and heavy leather gloves were at his belt. There were nicks in his heavy vest and his hands had bruised and torn knuckles. He stayed at the queen's other side and watched the entire tent, apparently uninterested in Nessar.

~~~~~~~~~~~~~~~~~~~~

Queen Deborah again addressed him, "Prince Nessar, we are honored to be here and want to show our recognition of our friendship by presenting you with goods from our land."

Deborah stopped and took a deep breath after she had looked up at the prince and found him continuing to stare. "How rude", her thoughts turned quickly. She was changing her opinion of this lecherous prince, but she had to get to Balthazar so she said nothing.

By this time, Jabael was convinced that Nessar was who he said he was and this wasn't a ransom situation. As he waited to be introduced he was studying the look on the prince's face. He saw that it was not lust, but astonishment and not just a little fear. He steadied his mother's arm, to get her attention. Debra refocused and as she looked at the prince again, he seemed to pull his gaze back to his guests as the introductions continued and Jabael had finally been presented. However, Nessar said nothing.

Then no one spoke as Nessar looked into the distance. Seconds passed. The royal attendants exchanged uncomfortable glances; then as time stretched out, they shifted on their feet and looked questioningly at each other and their masters once more. Deborah looked sideways at her son, who had continued to study Nessar; however, he still steadied her with a comforting hand.

Prince Nessar had been waiting for some response from the two mighty angels. They didn't address him, and no one mentioned them, so he just didn't know what was appropriate to do.

He seemed to finally come to his senses, "Welcome, welcome all. Please, thank you for the kind gifts and know that I am at your service. Your majesties, please allow us to take you and your. . .uh, others to your husband. He is not well, I am afraid."

Prince Jabael inclined his head slightly, "We thank God and we thank you for rescuing him. We are forever in your debt."

They left the tent; Prince Nessar paused because he was unsure of what to do. He was very aware that no one mentioned the angelic attendants and he surely didn't want to accidently turn his back to them. They didn't look so much threatening as they simply looked powerful and their very presence meant something very special.

Of course, he had never actually seen an angel before but he observed how Queen Deborah was acting and he began to believe that the angelic presence was not unusual for them. "Is this another part of being magi? That you grow used to angels?"

Deborah could not keep her feet from rushing to the tent where Balthazar was lying. Illya had listened to their arrival but didn't leave his master's bedside. He hurried to the entrance to the tent and as Deborah saw him, she touched his shoulder and they exchanged looks that told her much of her husband's condition. Then she was at Balthazar's side. Illya had cleaned him of the dirt and blood that had covered him; he had his lounging robes on and the prince's own surgeon was washing his head wounds.

Deborah glanced at the surgeon and he stepped back and slowly shook his head, Balthazar seemed to have slipped back into unconsciousness. She knelt at the bedside and swept her eyes over her husband as she leaned close to whisper in his ear.

"Balthazar, my beloved, I am here; you are safe. Your son is here too, please come back to us."

Prince Jabael stood regally and after pausing at the foot of the cot, he went to stand at Balthazar's other side. He examined the obvious wounds to assess if it was or was not an assassination attempt. Nothing he saw looked as though his father had been attacked; he then motioned Illya to him and stepped away from the bedside.

Still, the angelic visitors remained.

Prince Nessar stood at the entrance, he wanted to stay to see if he could be of any help but he was still confused about protocol. "What is expected? Should I mention the angels or should I stay silent?" As if in answer to his question, the angels both turned slightly toward the opening of the tent and as they did, the one nearer to him looked directly into his eyes for a moment and then spoke."

"Prince Nessar of Egypt, Almighty God knows of your act of compassion and will reward you according to His riches. Your love of mercy is highly regarded and because of your great heart, you have been chosen to welcome another group that will flee into the desert to you."

During that one moment, when their eyes met, time stopped. Prince Nessar saw and felt a wonderfully refreshing golden light cover him. He could actually feel, like sunlight, the absolute goodness that came from the angels and heard the voices of the ages all speaking to him. He staggered as the moment ended as if he had been held upright by that goodness.

Then the other angel turned again to the tent opening just as the sounds of footsteps were heard and Melchior and Caspar were led inside.

"Deborah, Deborah! You are here! We came as soon as we received the messenger," began Melchior as he gathered Deborah to her feet and covered her cold shaking hands with his own. He had long been one of Balthazar's confidants and a frequent guest; he was like family. Only he was aware of how much stress and strain she had been under and how afraid she was for her husband.

After quick greetings, Caspar went straight to Jabael to discuss what he knew with him. Since no one person had all of the history and information they needed time to help Balthazar, it was important that they agree to share the pertinent details. He paused as he looked again at Deborah;

there seemed to be a glow around her. "I wonder" he thought, "just how strong her spiritual powers are." He and the angels exchanged glances, "She seems to have brought help."

They all stayed close to Balthazar's side and what should be done and what things were in his best interests to do. It seemed likely that Balthazar would need to be transferred home, somehow. In his condition, he was just too ill to continue on; even if he did start to recover. And he hadn't.

Deborah told Melchior and Caspar everything about Balthazar's anxieties and how they sometime affected him. They reviewed for her what had been done for him and they compared notes and treatments for the various ailments that they had diagnosed in Balthazar. They spoke about the sleeplessness, the anxieties, the confusion and finally his flight away from the household and the time in the desert.

Then the surgeon spoke of the small shepherd that had defended Balthazar and because of him, their master was alive. Melchior of course knew the boy and understood the situation when they said the boy did not want to stay and rest, but as soon as Illya had arrived, he had gathered his lost and scattered sheep and had returned to their caravan.

They needed to find out what had happened, so Melchior sent for the boy and included a message that he would be required to return to his flocks afterward. He made sure that he was told that during his absence, two or three other boys would be needed to watch the fields.

The magi introduced themselves, belatedly to Nessar, "Thank you for the invitation to your caravan. We are pilgrims, Melchior of Persia and Caspar of India, and we thank you also for your goodness in rescuing our friend."

Nessar bowed his head and responded, "I am deeply honored. Please, welcome. Anything I have I share with you. I know of you and your families, my father the king would have me welcome you with all honor. Our countries have shared many centuries of friendship. Please tell me how I can help you and let me provide you with anything you need to further help King Balthazar."

"Thank you, we have brought medicines and droughts. If we may further consult with your surgeon, then we can make future plans for his care."

As Prince Nessar was preparing to leave the tent, he signaled to his servants to do as the magi requested. His caravan would stay still until there was news about Balthazar's condition. Perhaps during this time he could find out why the heavenly visitors were accompanying the family and he wondered more and more about the magi's pilgrimage to greet a newborn king.

Illya and Deborah were still conferring about Balthazar as Melchior and Caspar started examining Balthazar with the surgeon. Soon, Jabael addressed the prince, "Sire, is there somewhere that I may take my mother in order to be refreshed? We are quickly having our shelters put up but I feel that she may need to rest before then."

"Of course, at your desire, please have her and her attendants come to the next tent—it is small but I think she will be comfortable." Prince Nessar looked questioningly back at the angels and in response Jabael glanced over his shoulder. Funny he thought, Nessar again looks as though he sees something I don't.

After he had indicated the available inner rooms for Deborah's use, he continued, "Please allow me to serve you if there is anything else you". . .everyone in the room looked over at him when he broke off his speech. He was staring, again. They all turned to see a beautiful golden light spill across the room and the angelic messengers that had been so quiet stepped into the center of the room and started to speak.

"We come in the name of the Lord God Almighty! Hear His words."

Week 22

Messengers

Q ueen Deborah knew her heavenly visitors had been
present since they left the palace and she also knew
her son had not been aware of them. Over the years, she had
seen many angels and knew they served Almighty God and
were there for His purposes. As several others in her family,
she had the gift of "sight" but she also had the gift of a soul
that worshipped the Lord.

Nessar's eyes widened as the angels stepped forward;
he of course had seen them all along, but Jabael hadn't. He
visibly jumped into a defensive position with his hand at his
short sword but stopped and looked at his mother when she
gently put her hand over his. She gazed intently up at the
angels while obviously waiting for them to continue.

The angel proclaimed, "The Holy Son of the Lord God
Almighty will soon be born into the world and you, Prince
Nessar, have been chosen as one to protect the Child of God!
You will find that your kingdom will have a time of peace and
prosperity; you will no longer need to live at the edge of your
land. So, according to the will of God, return to the home of
your fathers in Egypt and build your palace there."

The other angel spoke and Deborah bowed. "Rise Queen
Deborah, greetings! Your Lord God is honored by your compassion and love. He has seen your acts of mercy and is
delighted to bless you by answering your prayers. You will

have only health and happiness in your family and you will grow old basking in their love."

Finishing, the messengers stepped back, looked up at the heavens and then disappeared, taking with them that amazing golden light. Jabael was still looking up where the messengers had been when he asked, "Mother, what did he mean?"

She clearly heard the words of her Lord and understood what gifts she had just been given. All of her chains of anxiety fell off of her and she breathed deeply. "First, send a rider back to the palace, your sister is well. Tell her that her father has recovered completely."

Jabael just stared. He knew their father was not well; in fact, the very opposite. What was going on?

Deborah continued, "He meant that your father's illness was intended to bring us together to hear these words. Prince Nessar will have a part in the kingdom of the Newborn. We weren't told details, but that part is clear."

"But how do you know these things?" Jabael started, "Did you hear them?"

"I heard them by faith. Have faith, Jabael."

~~~~~~~~~~~~~~~~~~~~

Nessar had obviously heard the message and because he was aware of the politics and petty battles going on within the huge land of Egypt, he understood what the angel meant. Egypt was large and prosperous and contained many kingdoms, but it was ultimately ruled by Pharaoh. It was to Pharaoh's advantage to keep the kingdoms squabbling against each other, so there seemed to be unending strife. Nessar was destined to rule his family's kingdom but that would be under the watchful eye of Pharaoh. His duty to his family during his lifetime would be to keep his kingdom intact; and by ruling wisely, he would make it larger and more prosperous so his family could continue to be safe.

~~~~~~~~~~~~~~~~~~~~

In Balthazar's tent, the magi had worked with the prince's surgeon to examine and redress Balthazar's head wound. It had stopped bleeding but the next problem was the swelling. Deborah had returned and was speaking to him softly and he seemed to hear her, he was quiet and looked comfortable but displayed no emotion nor did he speak.

A servant appeared at the entrance to say the shepherd was there. Illya went to the front of the tent to bring him to the magi.

The boy was so small. He was slightly built and the skin on his head and face had healed from an obviously terrible wound, one that had taken his sight. What it didn't take was the boy's spirit, he still had his rod and staff in his hand, which he immediately placed on the floor, and he stood very still, although very frightened at the attention he was getting.

He didn't want to be left behind because it was thought his blindness made him unable to work. He just wanted to go back to his job of living with and caring for the flock. He was ready to beg for that.

He bowed his head awkwardly and then he heard the warm, healing voice of King Melchior, one the magi. "Shepherd boy, you are truly the good shepherd. We have heard reports that we have you to thank for the return of your king Balthazar."

Deborah was at Balthazar's side and had turned, remembering the excited little boy that had left with the caravan. She swallowed hard as she saw the evidence of the great injuries and the resulting blindness.

"We truly thank you," she said. "Without you, I know my husband would still be lost, and who knows what else. But tell me, please, how did my husband happen out in the desert when he was so ill?"

The boy started to tremble; he had to convince them that he had no part in anything wrong. He raised his head and blurted out everything, "Mistress, I don't know! I was out with the flocks, that's where I stay and I saw they were being frightened. My lady, most people think that sheep are dumb; well they are, but sometimes they know things before we do.

We were out in the desert and they were frightened—at first I thought there was a wild animal nearby. So, I gathered the ewes together and went to the front of the flock, but there was another problem. If the wild animals were close, I knew I should have heard them by then."

"Shepherd, are you saying that you hear wild animals as they are coming toward the flock?" asked Melchior.

"Sire, since my eyes are. . .gone, I can hear many more things than I used to. Sometimes I hear them, other times I just know when something is near."

"Go on."

"My lady, the flock was scared but I couldn't hear anything. Then I smelled it, what was scaring them; I smelled blood. Then I heard breathing. I started searching and I found a man at the bottom near the rocks, he did call when he saw me; that is how I found him. He was covered in sand and blood was everywhere.

My lady, I didn't have any time to think about what to do, I took one of the cloths I carry for newborns and wrapped it around where I thought the blood was flowing from. That's when I heard the wild animals. So I stood up with my rod, but just then the guards found us, and scared the hyenas away."

He was finished with his story. He couldn't think of anything to add so he stood there with his chest heaving. He was as scared as he had been out in the desert.

Deborah stood and walked over nearer, "You are a brave boy; no, you are a brave man. We owe you your king's life, what can we do for you?"

"Majesty, I want nothing except to tend the sheep; to stay and to be with the flock."

"Would you not want something for yourself? And maybe a job inside the palace instead of out in the fields?"

"No, he would not. He is a shepherd." Deborah's surprise turned into a radiant smile as she looked back at her husband who had answered her question.

Jabael was first to his side, then the others and of course, Deborah, his most treasured wife. "You are back!"

And with that, the boy was given the job of shepherd for good. There would no longer be any chance that he would be left behind or be replaced with a healthier boy. He bowed quickly in thanks and straightened with a big smile on his face.

Balthazar looked weak, and was still very sick but he also looked peaceful and confident. He would no longer be terrorized by doubts and fears. He was miraculously healed of his fears and they seemed to have been replaced with faith.

"Master Shepherd, come closer." The boy quickly bowed to his Queen then ran to Balthazar's side. "Do you know that I believe you have a message for me? From where I was, I could hear your holy messenger. I understand it; I understand that the Newborn has revealed himself to you and you believe. You are blessed. So, tell me what our God would have me to know."

The boy was standing up very straight in front of the prone Balthazar. He had been scrubbed hard and clothed in his best in order to come into the king's presence. He had on his best cloak that was second- or third-hand, it still had some of the rusty brown color in the rough fabric but it was mostly very faded. It was spotless, however and that said a lot about the boy because where would he go to clean anything? His gown seemed to have been white at one time but a long history of holding ewes and frightened sheep had left his it mostly gray. His hands were rough and his feet bare, and at this moment he was the Almighty God's messenger to Balthazar.

He stood up tall and looked straight toward Balthazar for the first time, "He said 'Do not be anxious. You need not fight the battle that is the Lord God's. He goes before you. It is won."

Balthazar looked at the boy for a long time while he thought of these words and during that time, they healed him. He had been afraid; yes, afraid that the Newborn would demand his lands as tribute and the kingdom would be lost.

"I know now that he wants more from me. How will I answer Him?" Balthazar was deep in thought and almost didn't notice that everyone had turned to look at him. His anxieties had fallen away, his mind was healed and he was clear-headed. He seemed to be calm; it had to be a miracle!

He straightened up on his cot, "Shepherd, thank you for saving my life and thank you also for bearing this message. We will speak again. Now, I believe you have a job to return to. Illya, have a rider take him back."

"Majesty" and with that, the shepherd bowed and left his king's side to return to the field.

Week 23

Balthazar is Well

B oth Melchior and Caspar were astounded at the change in Balthazar. They had been at his side and bathing his wounds but this healing was about much more than his physical needs, his soul was saved.

"I'm feeling better now, I have to regain my strength because soon the star will continue its journey and we must be ready. And my beloved Deborah, do you mean to travel with us? In caravan?

Illya, prepare a meal and soon I will feel well enough to go back to our camp." Illya was staring at his master in amazement, he had been so afraid that he would never see him alive again; but he definitely was alive! He jumped as his name was mentioned and hastily bowing, took a minute to possessively clasp Balthazar's hand before he took off to find the very best of the food available.

Melchior placed his hand on Balthazar's forehead; he felt his clear and calm mind. He smiled, "Balthazar, welcome back. I believe Caspar and I need to return to the caravan. I can only imagine that you will be ready to travel before long and we have much to do.

Caspar finished speaking to Jabael and turned to Balthazar, "I look forward to seeing you soon my friend. We will have many pleasant discussions." Then both men and their attendants left the tent to speak to their host, Prince Nessar, before they returned to their own caravan.

Deborah sat near the head of the bed and spoke quietly for a while with her husband. Occasionally she would glance over at her son reclining. There would be time later to think on the things her husband was telling her that he had heard from the angels, but for now she was overcome with thanksgiving.

Balthazar continued, "The shepherd boy, he has a gift. He told me of the visit by the angel who strengthened him. And it has to be true; he is mighty in his own way. When I was broken and almost dead in the desert, he found me and as he bound my wounds, he talked to me. He brought me back from the darkness by his words. Amazing words; they held promises that he had heard from the angels. This simple boy, a child! He knows of things that we magi have studied and tried to understand for a thousand years. He knows the newborn King.

No, it is true, and it is more than just knowing *of* Him, he knows Him. We must go to worship Him, and also to know Him also. And the shepherd told me that he knows my friend Shadrach lives. He lives by his faith in the Newborn and will have a special place in His kingdom. But I will see him again on this earth.

Week 24

Back at the Caravan

P rince Nessar extended an invitation, "King Balthazar, you are welcome to stay as long as you would like. We are honored. I also have many questions about this wondrous star in the sky. Neither I nor my household interpreted its news and I know it has meaning for me, also."

Prince Nessar spent time with Balthazar everyday, listening to his ideas and asking about his theories. They spoke of truth and the heavenly messengers and just what this royal Newborn would conquer and where He would reign.

The following week the magi were on one of their daily visits to Balthazar, who was still recuperating at Nessar's caravan.

"Don't worry, it's true I'm feeling much better but I know I am not fully well. I will take things very slowly," Balthazar assured Caspar and Melchior as they stood at the entrance of the tent where Balthazar was sitting at his desk. However, it's time for me to come back, I believe our journey must resume.

So tell me; where is our star and does it still wait?"

Taking a deep breath of relief, Melchior said "This is indeed a miracle, Balthazar. As for the star, it seems to be waiting for you! It is still shining in the heavens, but not moving at all. Let's get you back to our camp and we can make plans."

Before moving Balthazar on a liter back to their camp, Balthazar and Deborah had called their son to their side, and then spoke with Prince Nessar. "There will be an alliance between our two nations, one that will eventually ensure both nations ask for a treaty with the Newborn's kingdom." They already knew Egypt would somehow be a guardian for the infant.

Balthazar returned back to the magi's camp and the Prince's caravan continued its trek as dusk settled. Melchior and Caspar were in Balthazar's tent and planning their nightly search of the heavens, "I am truly much better now, please don't worry about me," Balthazar stated again.

Caspar objected, "You are our dear friend and colleague. You can't stop us from being concerned for you."

Melchior added, "He means that we are so glad to find you well."

"And alive," smiled Balthazar.

"Yes, alive but tell us. What happened when you were out in the desert? And what happened to make you well?"

Balthazar sat up on the divan, still being tended closely by Illya,

"A miracle, no less! I had been tangled in a web of depression for days and I thought I would soon be fine. But it became much worse; I don't know what I thought I was going to do by leaving the camp and wandering in the desert.

I was confused and disoriented when I walked away, and it became worse as I walked. When I slipped and fell, I thought I was going to die. I could not move my arms and legs and I could feel the blood dripping out of my head onto my neck and back.

And I was glad! I didn't want to live, I am very sorry to say.

Then, as I was lying face down in agony on the sand and hoping to die soon, I heard bells. I know now that they were the bells on the sheep in our flocks, but then they sounded beautiful. I heard the shepherd's voices; I know it sounds like I am confused but I can remember hearing two distinct voices and I know there was only one small boy that was there.

I clearly heard a shepherd's voice that was deep and kind to the sheep; He spoke to his own and then continued and also spoke to those who are lost. It sounds odd to say this now, but it is simply the truth.

He said that He is the good shepherd and He will give His life for all. I can still hear that melody of his voice in my mind and it is beautiful. I won't ever forget it but even though He was just talking to sheep; I have come to believe He was also speaking to me." Balthazar realized this sounded crazy and strained forward, "And I know He was really there, I'm not crazy."

Melchior and Caspar were both seated near and leaned in, "Balthazar, we believe you. Really, don't be distressed, please tell us the rest."

"As I said, I know He was there with me. I felt him close to me; but I never saw him, but it was only because I was face down in the sand and the blood was all over me. As I felt him nearby I could hear the shepherd boy slowly coming closer to the spot that I lay, but the boy didn't know I was even there. He was searching for what was frightening the sheep.

As the boy came closer, I felt, no I heard the Shepherd speaking to him, telling him which path to take to get to me. Then He placed gentle hands on me that stopped most of the bleeding from my head. As he turned me over, I tried to open my eyes to look into His face, but I couldn't, and then the shepherd boy appeared."

So I know He was there with me, but I never saw Him; I didn't see Him at all. But He saved me; I am alive because of Him, the Good Shepherd."

Week 25

Melchior

The Prince of Egypt had left to continue on his journey. Back at their campsite, the magi set about their routines in order to allow Balthazar time to recuperate and rest. He seemed different in ways that were hard to describe; he was assured and acted as though his recent illness and almost lethal fall in the desert were planned to bring him only good.

Melchior noticed Deborah watching Balthazar closely; but saw that she only listened to him and never seemed distressed.

Melchior returned to his tent to rest during the heat of the day but before he allowed his servant to draw the purple covering over the entrance, he assembled his star maps. Maybe when nighttime came tonight, they would find answers in the heavens. He wanted another sign to show them when and where they should be traveling to find the Newborn. The star hadn't moved in days, it waited. Soon, perhaps, it would continue its journey so they could continue theirs. He picked up a small book and turned to his cot.

Melchior opened the first page of the journal after he swung his legs onto the bed and lie back. It was filled with writings he had collected over his lifetime, prophecies he had discovered and carefully researched that spoke of the Messiah and His coming. Melchior's family were not Jews, he was born far from anywhere the Jewish people had ever traveled; but he knew their history, that of slaves.

But the promised Messiah was to be born a Jew; prophets had clearly foretold His coming for hundreds of years. Melchior had always been drawn to the story, and as he grew older and spent more time studying the prophecies, he believed in the Messiah and he became aware he was to have a part in the life of the Messiah. And the truths he sought were in Him.

Did he believe the Messiah was of God? *Yes.*

What else did he know about the Messiah? *Not much.*

He knew He was coming to create His own kingdom. However, he knew that in order to establish a new kingdom, there would be revolution, war, and domination of whole countries. Melchior sighed heavily, the fight for power would cause so much misery for everyone involved, and so who was this Newborn?

Melchior needed to know because being a ruler himself, if this newborn king was so strong and so all-powerful that His kingdom would rule the world, Melchior knew he must present himself as soon as possible in order to align himself with this powerful Messiah for the good of his own country.

Somehow Melchior thought this King of kings would be different, the prophecies foretold the coming kingdom of the Messiah that was full of His power and majesty and his great mercy and forgiveness. That didn't sound like a conquering warrior. Maybe this kingdom would be filled with knowledge and understanding; and if so, he hoped he could share in this understanding.

Now he believed the Messiah would hold the key to this and all knowledge. Prophecies agreed that the King would be all-powerful and then they seemed to say that he would give his life for those He loves. This is where Melchior was sure he had this all wrong. After all; what all-powerful king would choose to die for those in his kingdom?

So he studied the Messiah and searched for truth. As he learned, he felt himself changing. He found truth and he longed to know this Newborn and be part of His kingdom. He was unsure of this part, however; because if he wanted to be part of the Newborn's kingdom, would he be accepted? He was afraid he wasn't good enough.

Week 26

Caspar

The order came and the caravan immediately responded. The camp that had been their home for weeks suddenly disappeared, replaced by a long line of laden camels and flocks being herded together. Everyone excitedly went about their jobs in record time, the sounds of camels braying and people talking and laughing spilled out over the desert floor.

Finally everything was ready and there seemed to be a breathless pause. The magi had been standing together checking their charts and maps, and then they agreed on the plan for the night. After a searching look at the evening sky that held the glittering star riding toward the east, Balthazar's command sailed upon the wind, "We move."

The twilight slipped quickly into night and the caravan moved steadily through the cool darkness. The sand still held the heat from the day but was rapidly giving it up, causing those tending the camels to draw their scarves around their heads and necks. The beacon could easily be seen as it moved ahead to guide them.

It was a few hours before everyone calmed down to their tasks. Occasionally there was a raised voice that was quickly answered in a hush and then the expanse of the desert swallowed any further sound.

The magi rode together as usual toward the front of the caravan, where they would frequently speak softly to each other, and then could be seen nodding their heads in agreement.

Caspar soon asked his servant for his scrolls, he found he could read the maps by the light of the royal star. He pondered the area in the west that they seemed to be traveling toward and was eager to find to which royal family the Newborn belonged.

Caspar was the oldest son of the ruling family; he was tall and slim and known as one of the rare magi who had the gift of prophecy; he could see into the future. He attracted many offers of marriage from all over the known world but was not interested. He felt he was searching for something just out of his reach; in truth, he didn't know what he was searching for.

His family was wealthy, even by royal standards and they were generous. They were able to keep Rome at a distance because of their many friendships with just about every country in the region. No one would agree, under any circumstances, to align themselves against India.

Caspar and Balthazar's families had been allied for decades and they were encouraged to be friends since they were children. As a very young child, Caspar often had what he then called daydreams. He could see and speak to people that others couldn't see and these people told him things. His grandfather was a royal mage and knew immediately that his grandson was blessed with great powers of prophecy, even as a child. He was determined that this child would take the path of a mage, and set about mentoring him. He taught Caspar that he held great power but with this great power was great responsibility, especially since he would also inherit the crown.

Unlike Balthazar who studied warfare in order to be a warrior king, Caspar developed his intuitive abilities and found a love of truth. He established one of the largest centers of learning in the world and encouraged culture and academia. Through him, his land had become a center of education and freedom of thought. In time, he had become a full mage, he was learned and had exceedingly strong insights that he easily found he could translate into prophecy.

Caspar had found there was so much for him to learn and to understand in order to be a good ruler. This knowledge humbled him and he strived to be the good ruler he felt he was learning to be.

He was sitting on his camel meditating on these matters when he saw a vision; he had learned these were a precious gift for him to learn from. So, he breathed a prayer of thanksgiving as the vision unfolded before him and then he looked around eagerly.

The river was large. It flowed quickly in the middle and had several wide areas that collected on the sides that were looked like places shallow enough in which to gather water, wash clothes or maybe bathe.

He saw children playing at the sides of the river near a village, and he had to smile; they were trying to catch fish with their hands and one industrious small girl was using her shawl to scoop them up. Good for her!

Down the river, there were fewer and fewer villages and the water continued to travel miles in the bright sunlight. Caspar could see well-worn paths beside the river and sometime there would be people traveling on them.

Further still, the river took a bend and there were giant rocks that had been carved out of the bank by the river and because of them, the water was held still and it was quiet there. A large group of men, women and children could be seen gathered there and they were listening to a speaker who was more than hip-deep in the water.

"I am the voice calling in the wilderness to all who will listen! The Holy One of God Almighty has come to gather all to Himself, He is the Son of the Most High! He is calling all to listen to Him and to be saved by Him. He offers His gift of life, for free, to all who will follow him."

The man spoke with a mighty voice, the sound thundered off of the rocks and the water. It could easily be heard by those on the riverbank and those still walking.

Caspar took a closer look at the man speaking, he looked like a hermit! He didn't look educated nor did he look like anyone of influence. He was dressed in some sort of animal skin and he was the color of a nut, scoured by the desert sun and wind. However, he spoke with the power of knowledge and authority.

Meanwhile someone called out, "What should we do in order to obtain His gifts?"

The man turned his piercing gaze upon the man and answered "Confess your sins to him! Change the way you live and love each other! Obey His Word and He will give you the gifts He has promised through the words of the prophets."

Several in the crowd seemed to understand and Caspar could hear their voices. Then one man called out in a humble voice, "I want to follow him. I want to obey His Word."

The man in the water had never taken his gaze off of the man on the bank, and as the man responded, he immediately answered, "Then come into the water, now; be baptized and believe in Him."

The man hesitated, clearly about to back away, "He won't want me. I'm outcast. I'm a murderer."

The group on the bank murmured in surprise and visibly moved away from him. The parents gathered close to the children that had been playing in the crowd, and then all waited to see what would happen next.

The man in the river took notice and for a minute looked sad, "Confess your sin and your sorrow for that sin. Repent! I tell you that He is faithful! He will hear your prayer and look into your heart; He has the power and He will save you and give you life."

The man fell onto his knees and covered his face with his hands, weeping and praying. After a minute, his shoulders straightened and he raised his head. His face looked different, he was strong and peaceful; he rose and stepped into the water. He made his way to the man, they talked for a moment, then the man in the water nodded and pronounced, "I, John, baptize you, Shadrach, in the name of the Son of the Almighty God" and he dipped him under the surface.

Caspar stared into space, wanting to see every detail that he was being shown. He of course knew Shadrach; he had been cast out into the desert and thought to be dead! Caspar knew beyond any doubt that he was alive.

The vision drew him back. There was another. There was one who was standing very still in the water; he looked like someone that was yet to come. Caspar could almost see through the figure and then He turned and looked straight at Caspar. "Do you believe? Are you willing to follow me?"

Week 27

Caspar's Prophecy

Melchior and Balthazar were at Caspar's side, "He's back. Are you all right? Can you speak?" Illya was bending over him, offering a sip of cool water."

Of the magi, Caspar had the strongest gift of prophecy and sight. It wasn't unusual for him to be able to "see" the future or people and things miles away. It wasn't painful for him, but his body sometimes seemed to just stop during the "sight". He often chuckled to himself, he must look dead at these times and so it rightfully scared those who came upon him.

Caspar felt as though he had been far away, he looked at his hands that were gripped together and he barely recognized them, "He lives, do you know that? I saw him and he follows the Newborn that we seek."

Balthazar didn't hesitate but nodded saying; "Deborah has told me she believes Shadrach is alive. Where is he? He seeks the Newborn?"

Deborah had moved over to Caspar and placed a comforting hand on his arm as she encouraged him to continue, "It was an amazing vision, I saw Shadrach and a prophet who was proclaiming the Newborn as King of kings and Lord of lords just as the angels have said. I saw Shadrach; he is alive, but the prophet. . .the prophet will be alive, but he isn't quite yet; he will proclaim the Newborn in the future."

Deborah smiled at her husband as he sagged in relief with the news.

"Where do we go? Does this tell us anything we need to know now?"

"We will continue to follow the star" stated Melchior. "This is information that I believe we will need in the future; but for now, we continue to follow."

The caravan moved through the desert as the night deepened and after a while, those that were riding had quieted and those walking had found companions to walk with as they kept the camels going forward. The supplies that the whole caravan lived on were secure in the middle of the line; the camels ambled along as they liked, the flocks were being carefully herded by the shepherd boy, and soon, only occasional whispers were heard.

However, Caspar stayed awake and alert, thinking of what he had seen. He was happy to know Shadrach lived and he was sure they would meet again. He found that he wanted to know more and more about the Newborn and His kingdom. He now knew beyond any doubt in his heart that He was more than just another king that would conquer and rule over a squabbling part of the desert. Caspar believed this King would reign over much more than he had originally believed.

Caspar knew that earthly royalty, himself and the other magi included, were anointed by God to lead their people. Now Caspar learned this King would reign over all men, everywhere; and he just didn't understand that concept. In fact, only the Romans believed they could and should rule others beside themselves; and they did that through conquest and their own military might. Their very bloody military might.

This Newborn would be God, anointed by Himself and would rule in truth and through peace. Caspar shook his head; he just couldn't understand the thought.

Week 28

Visions

🙚

F resh pink sunlight appeared at the edge of the desert, this was the sign that the caravan would soon stop. It finally settled alongside another set of travelers just inside the green oasis. Guards had ridden ahead earlier to find space at the oasis and secure the area. Just as the weary travelers came within view of the campsite, the desert was heating up and the sun seemed to be getting unbearably bright.

Colorful tents seemed to bloom almost immediately and animals were groggily gathered together in the shade for safety and rest. Food and drink had already been served, and now, secure for the day, most of the people in the caravan crept inside or underneath shelters to sleep.

The magi took another look at the gleaming star and as they did, it started its marvelous transformation that they saw each morning. It changed it shape from the giant star form by first methodically telescoping in its horizontal arms, then filling out its middle shape by moving its vertical beams alongside to fill out the middle.

They bent their heads together once again to chart the star's progress before they settled in to rest during the scorching day. Balthazar summoned the shepherd boy and talked to him about the Newborn that they all were traveling to honor. He asked him to tell him again about his remarkable vision.

"The golden angel told me that a King is to be born and that this King is the Son of the Most High God! So I bowed down and I was very scared. He told me that the Newborn loves me and has been born on earth for me and that I am one of his sheep in his flock. I understand that because I know how much I love each one of these that I care for, even the ones that give me trouble. He also told me that I have been given a very special job. I just kept quiet but then I raised my face so they would know they were talking to the wrong boy because I am just a shepherd and a blind one, "I'm sure I can't help you, I am certainly not the one you want.

You see, I didn't expect the Newborn King to care about me or save me from anything. But the angel said to me, 'You shall know Him, though He is King of all, He was born in a stable. And He will surely save you and everyone that follows Him.'"

Balthazar knew that the boy had heard correctly when he said the King was born in a stable. But he didn't think a real stable; maybe stable meant something else in another country. So what and where was the King's birthplace and how would they find Him? The boy said they would find Him, and they would know Him.

"Thank you for sharing these words with me, shepherd. I will remember them; then shortly after that, the boy returned to his sheep.

As he left, Caspar was in his tent and he had another vision; he saw the boy settled against a hillside along with other shepherds who were guarding their sheep. It was night-time and there was their royal star—shining brightly above the valley. He could see each one of the shepherds faces as they were settling in for the night; frequently one would get up to coax one of his animals back to the flock and then return to lie down.

Then the star started to move and it seemed to dance in the sky and as it flashed, the sky became filled with angels! He could see them! Thousands upon thousands—and they were all singing along with beautiful music. Then their voices seemed to become music, and they both merged in the most amazing joyous sounds that he had ever heard!

They sang "Glory to God in the Highest!" and the love in their song echoed from the hilltops through every valley. They were celebrating the very birth of the King of kings and one of the angels appeared above them in a blaze of golden light and spoke to the shepherds!

"Arise! The Son of God, King of Kings had been born! You are to go into the city of Bethlehem, to a stable, to welcome and to worship Him."

Caspar saw the angels return to heaven and the shepherds were still on the hillside in shock. All at once the boys broke out in smiles, clapping each other on the back and then stood up to do exactly as the angel had bid them. Caspar also saw their shepherd boy, he had been gazing up at the angels; and he turned his face to his companions that were celebrating, and looking at them, smiled back.

He could see!

Week 29

The Village

C aspar smiled in return and said nothing, but was determined to keep all of this in his heart and mind.

The maps they had were the best available and so they were able to avoid most hostile areas and to find the best oases to rest during the scorching days. They had been exceptionally lucky. They had not had to fight off thieves except when they had first started and that skirmish was easily won, thanks to the soldiers that guarded them.

Their maps now showed they were approaching a larger village that frequently resupplied caravans. They would need to stay several days, depending on how long it would take to get their supplies. They would make camp near the village, lists of supplies were ready, and the courier had just returned this night with money to pay those in the caravan who wanted an advance in order to go into the village and buy things for themselves.

Each mage eventually drifted to the coolness of his tent to sleep as the sun baked the earth around them during the day.

As the sun went down that evening, the caravan reorganized itself faster than usual. Everyone was eager to get to the village and see something different than miles and miles of sand. There would be people, stores, places to eat, and of course, other places that offered drink and entertainment.

At about halfway through the night, a rider returned to the moving caravan, "Your majesty, our scouts have reached the village and have sent word. It is two to three hours out and it is secure."

Balthazar acknowledged the information, "Thank you, I know we are all anxious to be in a village for a change," then he then made a note on the map. Looking up at their star, he marked again.

The magi each went to prepare and Balthazar talked to Illya to tell him of the timeframe. His servant then went to select the robes that his king would wear when they arrived. Balthazar left the front of the caravan as it settled outside of the village and was led to the royal tent that had already been erected. His hair and facial hair were carefully trimmed and then he was oiled and finally dressed in robes to reflect his station and importance.

~~~~~~~~~~~~~~~~~~~~

The caravan approached the village and the sounds of the excited travelers talking among themselves could be heard for miles in the desert. The magi were now dressed in magnificent robes; not the robes that they would wear when presented to the Newborn of course, but these were beautifully flowing tapestries that adorned their bodies while priceless diadems crossed their foreheads. Everyone, even the youngest child in this small village, would know these were very important men.

Scouts continued to ride into the village to announce the pending arrival of the magi's large caravan, and as they left, other riders were returning from their forward-missions.

"Soldier! Any problems?" Madai asked.

"No, Captain. Everything is in readiness for the caravan; we have located and secured a small oasis on the outskirts of the village. It is empty now and can easily accommodate our herds. As for the village, it is small so we will cause quite a stir when we arrive and they are very happy to sell us supplies."

"We are supposed to create a stir; this village has never had the privilege of entertaining royalty. Our masters will certainly want to talk to anyone that knows anything about the great star."

The captain rode back and reported to Balthazar who had returned to the front of the caravan. "Your highness, we are approaching the village and riders have found it safe and awaiting your arrival." Even though the caravan would camp in the oasis, he still completed his account with the traditional, "May we have your permission to enter?"

~~~~~~~~~~~~~~~~~~~~~

Balthazar was robed in two layers of silken garments, the first was a brilliant yellow and the second was draped at his shoulders and it was the color of fire. His golden diadem was snuggled down on his forehead. It had been determined that he would not wear the most opulent of his jewels; there was no reason. So he wore necklaces of gold that held strings of creamy pearls that each seemed exactly the same size. Both of his upper arms were circled by gold, and cuffs of hammered gold 5" wide were at his wrists. Marvelous precious stones in beautiful rings sparkled in the moonlight each time his hands moved.

The captain of the guard stood by Balthazar as they both watched Illya sulk away with armfuls of the most beautiful robes that had ever been seen. Illya looked unhappy, and he was, but he dared not argue further with his master. He never liked it when he thought Balthazar was dressed below his station. He had picked out the more beautiful, costly robes along with more jewelry for Balthazar, and as his body servant, Illya thought he knew what would be best for his master to wear. Balthazar had declined and Illya was now sulking.

He was returning the unworn robes to their chests in the caravan train and was talking to himself, "I feel I have done all I can to ensure that my master is dressed according to his royal station. It will not be my fault when these horrible peasants look straight through him and don't believe he is magi. My King Balthazar has never paid attention to his clothing; and now, what more can I do?

What's more, I will just look like another lowly servant to another lowly master when I, or we, should look like what we both really are."

Priscilla came over to help and together they placed the protected garments in their own chests and then returned the chests to the secure wagon. Often the seamstress teased Illya about his love of the colorful and fluid fabrics that were in Balthazar's clothing chests. He would arrange beautiful gowns for Balthazar and he would resolutely choose the more work-friendly, less exotic garments. Nevertheless, Illya always hoped for the brighter fabrics.

Working together smoothly, they both began to chat about the village and what they wanted to do. The seamstress had ordered supplies and knew they were waiting there, she wanted some dyes that were hard to find and she had sent stitching needles ahead in order for them to be sharpened. She was preparing to make the robes and other garments that her master would want when he was presented to the Newborn. She would, of course, make the final designs and then carefully sew the bejeweled fabrics as they got closer to their destination.

She was excited; she had never been within such a large caravan before and was happy to find that it seemed to be like a big family; that was always on the move. Some people became tired of the others, but not her; she liked the friend-ships she found and she enjoyed her job.

The two had finally found common ground and were now friends, they continued to speak as the riders coming and going had become constant. The caravan with its baggage, animals and herds had found the oasis and was quickly settling in place. The timing was perfect. The sky in the east had turned pink and they were set to enter the village just after its citizens rose for the day and were starting about their business.

"Yes, enter when you see fit," replied Balthazar to the caravan master and he glanced back to the other magi who were ready and waiting for the ride into the village. How different they looked.

The other two had been carefully dressed by their servants; they looked like the royal magi that they most certainly were. Their gowns and accessories were starting to sparkle as the sky brightened. Everyone in the village had heard of each of these men, they were magi who loved teachings and truth, and they searched the world in their quest. Now they were on pilgrimage to greet the King of Truth. Everyone had heard this remarkable story, everyone was always interested in what royalty were doing; and these were royal magi. Today they would witness their entrance into their village! They would be able to tell this story to their children and grandchildren about the day they actually saw one of these fabled men, when three royal magi came to their village.

~~~~~~~~~~~~~~~~~~~~~

Well, thought Balthazar, as he looked at his friends, I guess Illya was right; maybe in the future I need to give some thought to dressing up. He returned the smiles of his friends and turned to ensure his wife was safely in the place of honor in the parade out of the caravan, and then he rode forward into the village.

Their entrance was announced with the sound of horns and music, followed by several companies of guards. The guards wore the uniform of the households of the magi and they all kept weapons at their sides.

First, Melchior's procession entered, servants held great lengths of silken fabric that covered most of the street to shelter him from the heat of the rising sun. Villagers lined the small passageways to watch the households, to see the beautiful animals that were ridden, to be amazed at the opulence of royalty and finally, to buy and sell.

Melchior wore a golden gown that was partially covered with a golden robe that was made from golden thread with diamonds sewn in between that made the fabric shimmer and sparkle. It was breath-taking; he had a circlet crown on his head that showcased 20 large diamonds surrounded by gold and he was followed by his retinue who were clothed in their own priceless robes.

Caspar's household was next in the procession into the village. Even his servants were spectacular in that they wore priceless necklaces of gold around their necks that proclaimed the mage that they served. Shirtless servants arrayed in gold and wearing rainbow-hued pantaloons carried Caspar's liter. The mage himself was seated upon a gleaming liter with piles of silken pillows at his back. His skin shined with valuable oils; and instead of wearing a flowing robe, he was shirtless and wore pantaloons as did his bearers, but his were golden like the sun. Caspar outshone the rising sun; he could hear the sighs from the villagers as their bowed their heads at the sight of him!

After the first two magi passed, there was a show of their wealth, intended to impress and entertain the villagers. There were baskets and baskets of fragrant exotic flowers and plants. There were bolts of fabrics that floated on the breeze or shined like precious jewels. Finally, there were casks and casks of jewels on display.

Balthazar's household was last in this parade because he had the largest security force to march by and because he always traveled with so many of his favorites.

His favorite horses!

He dearly loved beautiful animals and his estate was known everywhere for horses that danced on the winds. Their beauty was legendary and so as he came into the village, he sat astride one of his beauties. The mare was not large, but exquisitely formed; she was strong and even stronger-willed. She was excited to be in the village and she loved the attention! She pranced; and then tossing her head, she playfully tried to pull the reigns from Balthazar's hands. Again and again he had to reseat himself; and then finally he just shook his head at her, while smiling all the time.

The appearances of the other two magi were impressive, but Balthazar's procession was show-stopping! He was attired in an emerald-hued gown that was fitted so he rode in comfort. His headpiece covered his head and trailed behind him and twinkled with emeralds of all sizes. His prize horses appeared next, each with a lead that matched his emerald-laden head-dress. At one point, one of the ponies slipped out of its sparkling lead and took off straight through the others toward him.

Balthazar turned just in time to see the pony dash past an older horse and then bump rudely into his own mare. He leaned over in an attempt to grasp the dangling lead when his mare smartly bite the offending pony on the ear and then pushed him back behind them with a shove of her hip. His favorite knew her place - at the front of the line! The villagers that had lined both sides of the procession cheered and clapped, they loved the horses! At the sound, she acknowledged them by tossing her head and prancing to the side.

The households had finally entered the village and were formally welcomed. The servants had already been bargaining and buying necessities and had found out the information that they needed in order to buy other items. Everyone was catching up on news and gossip.

Deborah had been part of the procession as it slowly made its way into town and she was now escorted to the inn where the royal family would stay. She would not see Balthazar until later. She was dressed in her finest robes; she knew the women of the village would judge her household according to her behavior and the quality of her gowns. She purposefully moved slowly and regally, acknowledging all she saw, touching hands as she went by. She wanted to shop in the village for items for herself and for her household, so she was eager to settle into the inn so she could slip out with her servant, her seamstress and however many guards they would be assigned.

There were real rooms instead of tents here at the inn; they were small, but clean and comfortable. She fully realized that these were the best accommodations in the village. After her visitors left and before the sun had gone halfway down in the sky, she left her rooms with her entourage to shop.

"Lady, I have seen the most beautiful fabrics for gowns. I believe you must see them!"

"Priscilla, that is just what I wanted, where are they?"

As they entered the marketplace, a village girl, eager to make a sale pressed close, "My lady, please let me guide you, I have lived in this village all of my life and I can show you to the best stores and get you the best prices."

"My lady only wants the very best, do you know *those* places?" asked Priscilla, glaring at the other girl.

"Please show us, and thank you," said Deborah as she looked askance at the seamstress. She knew Priscilla was looking for only the best, but she didn't have the gift of patience.

"Ah, such beautiful fabrics and what colors!" Deborah and the large group went from store to store and from one part of the marketplace to the next.

~~~~~~~~~~~~~~~~~~~~

The caravan's occupants had spilled out into the village, soon the cafes and the markets were filled and it was obvious that old friends were greeting each other. Many in the magi's caravan households were from small surrounding villages, so it was at times like this that the young men would be able to return however briefly to visit their families and hometowns.

They would have time to see families and sweethearts, so the few hours or days turned into large reunions. But, there was work to be done; supplies to be bought and loaded, and then repairs to be made. Animals were tended and the food stores for man and animals were resupplied.

By evening, most everyone took time away from their jobs and gathered with friends or family. Deborah and Balthazar were to be guests of the most prominent family in the village, the family that managed the olive groves. The family had supplied quality olive oil, for generations; to the royal household. Parents knew parents and their children played together.

Merriam, Deborah's maid, was draping a mist-like layer of fabric over Deborah's shoulders, "My lady, I need to ask Priscilla to make you some other gowns. See? This one is old."

"Oh, Merriam, how can you say that? I like this one. It is beautiful and it is one of my favorites!" Deborah looked in the mirror again, thinking she may see a flaw in the fabric.

"I can say that, your majesty because I think you have worn this before!"

"Of course I've worn this before; that's how it became one of my favorites."

"But it just won't do for you to wear old, worn out fabrics; it doesn't reflect your status, if I may say so."

"Merriam, you are a snob."

"Yes, my lady."

"You know; we will never get along. You just won't argue at all!"

She looked horrified, "My lady! Of course I wouldn't argue with you. It's not my place."

Deborah smiled to show that she was teasing, "Of course it is, and see; now you are finally arguing."

Merriam was slightly miffed but too disciplined to show it, "If I am a snob, my lady, it is because I want the world to be aware of the status of my lady Queen. You shouldn't be seen in less than the very best."

"Thank you, I will remember your words; but really, isn't this gown beautiful? And if I recall, you are the one who found this beautiful fabric and the seamstress that could work with it."

"Yes, and her family lives in the village. I want to go to their shop to see what new fabrics they have and the newest miracles of sewing that they have learned. I am excited that I may find something especially exquisite for your majesty, something to wear for the Newborn King."

"Doesn't this family have other sons and daughters? I seem to remember a son that you talked about?"

Merriam's face flushed a deep color of pink as Deborah talked on and on. "Oh my, are you well? You seem to be overheated."

"No, I am fine." The ladies that accompanied Deborah had congregated in the chamber and all laughed as Merriam tried to remain serious until finally she had to burst out laughing also.

"My lady, you have a good memory. May I go to see the family about purchases for you, when you leave for the evening?"

"Yes, go ahead;" started Deborah innocently, "what or maybe more importantly, who will you be looking for?"

The ladies all laughed as she again flushed brightly.

~~~~~~~~~~~~~~~~~~~~~

Soon afterward, the royal couple left for their evening, accompanied by their retinues. Merriam had placed jewels that sparkled like stars on Deborah's ears, neck and wrists and her rings included the fabled royal jewels. Her outer garment was stitched with golden threads and as she moved, all eyes turned to her.

Merriam approved, thinking "This is the attention my lady should always command." She thought again with pleasure, of the admiring look on her lord Balthazar's face when he came to collect Deborah.

At the same time, Balthazar looked handsome and perfectly royal. Illya had washed, manicured, oiled, powered, and/or combed him until he rebelled and ordered him to stop and bring his clothes. His hair had been washed in rose water and trimmed around his face then allowed to be longer at the sides and back so that it dropped onto his broad shoulders. His hands and feet still stung from the clipping and cuticle work that had Illya huffing and puffing dramatically. Illya took every opportunity to let Balthazar know that he felt his master refused to treat himself as royally as he should; he should be manicured and clothed regally everyday. Instead, his lord actually seemed to love to exercise and back at the palace would actually take part in training with Shadrach and the other soldiers. Illya couldn't understand this and clearly let Balthazar know that his acts of physical labor caused much more work for himself.

Illya was beside himself because he had full control over Balthazar's garments this evening. Priscilla and he had created the entire ensemble and together had prepared Balthazar.

His lord finally arrived to his wife's apartments dressed in a royal purple robe the color of an amethyst. The fabrics used in his inner gown were of the thinnest silk that lay close over his form; and over this was an outer gown of the same color but in heavy silk that moved slowly and, as Illya described, royally. He had amethysts the size of ostrich eggs at his headdress, wrists, and then displayed across his chest sewn onto his gown.

Balthazar thought that he looked overdressed for the night but caught himself as he was going to refuse the jewels.

He suddenly didn't have the heart to say no when he could see that Illya was so obviously happy. His face was alight and he couldn't seem to do enough to ready his lord. Thinking back, Balthazar realized he often irritably would tell Illya to just stop and leave him when he was trying to dress him in fine garments. Maybe this was something else he needed to learn. . .consideration. Then, he noticed the look of admiration and love on Deborah's face when he entered her apartments. And that was worth it all!

~~~~~~~~~~~~~~~~~~~~

As the sun set, the desert started to cool off quickly but the village was still bustling; the evening had started to draw long shadows. As adults talked in the marketplace, children ran around excitedly. Merriam had left the large stone inn soon after her lady had gone and she had finished tidied up. She knew the village and walked briskly to the edge of the marketplace. She found the home easily and as she arrived the door was flung open by the family. "Greetings! Come in, come in, Merriam! It is so good to see you again!"

She had brought gifts for each family member. They were eagerly accepted and gifts were in turn were given to her and then they all sat down to eat and to gossip, the local form of news. She was brought up to date on who was where, who had done what, what children had been born, and who was newly betrothed.

A lady's maid always had the best first hand information about what was going on in the royal household. This was a never-ending source of amazement to others; royalty lived so differently from other folks. Sometimes, of course, Merriam embellished, slightly but she didn't usually need to add anything.

Stories of what the magi were studying in the heavens and of the giant star that was guiding them to the Newborn King were told and all were amazed. Long into the night, her friends asked about the Newborn King, and she told them that she herself had seen the angels and had heard their proclamations that the one they seek is the Son of Almighty God and will establish His kingdom.

She continued, "The master said that this Royal Newborn has fulfilled every one of the prophecies that have been foretold about the Messiah."

She had seen the miracles, heard the stories and urged her friends to believe that the Newborn is the One of God and He had been born to search for and find those who are lost.

"He will establish His kingdom that will last forever", she declared. She spoke with authority received from the angels and from the magi. The family was breathless and asked her question after question.

Finally they looked at each other, and told her that they wanted to acknowledge the Newborn as Lord. What did they have to do?

She hesitated. Who was she to offer what the Newborn had come to establish?

However, she was overwhelmed with the feeling that this was the right thing for her to do. She told them everything she had heard and what she knew about the coming Newborn Lord and fell silent. She ended with, "When you pray, tell God that you believe the Royal Newborn is His Son and that you want him to be your Lord also." She felt emptied and at peace. She seemed to be resting in the news of the Son of the Almighty Lord.

Along with seeing this dear family, Merriam had been hoping to see someone else, also; their eldest son. She had met him when she had accompanied Deborah on a short trip and they stopped at the village once before. They had talked, and promises had been spoken. Where was he?

It would be unseemly to ask about him, so she was hoping to have some time privately with the daughter her age in the family—then she could ask.

It was almost time for her to go and her friend, Lidia, got up and said she wanted to show Merriam some of the handwork she had made and to ask her advice. Leaving the family to talk about all of the news, both ladies walked off to another side of the home.

Once out of view of the family, Lidia turned and gripped both of Merriam's hands in hers, "There is some terrible news that my parents just can't tell you. It is about my brother, Josheem."

"What has happened?" Lidia took her hand and pulled her into her room, and then placed her other hand on the door as she continued, "My. . ." She stopped.

Her mother was there in the doorway, "Merriam, your escort has arrived to take you back to the household."

"Thank you, I am on my way", she nodded her head and glanced searchingly at Lidia. What had happened? It seemed as though she wouldn't see Josheem. She knew he still lived, there was no sign that he had been injured or died and if there had been a wedding or a betrothal that would have been joyful news that the family would have shared. What had happened?

Lidia watched as her friend had to walk away and saw as she turned back to her with obvious questions in her eyes,

"Can I tell her? Or have I lost my nerve?" She thought to herself. She knew she had to be honest with her friend, but what if she just didn't understand? Would she be like everyone else?

Meanwhile Merriam had thanked her friends for the wonderful evening and dinner, then slipped a soft mantle over her head and silently left the house; she smiled up at her escort. Usually she was thankful that Deborah thought so much of her that she wanted her to be safe and therefore sent escorts to accompany her. Now, she didn't know what to think. She decided she would just have to go back later on her own and speak to Lidia.

As the two left and got to the end of the building and started to turn, there was a sudden rush from the end of the house. The escort was more soldier than courtier and firmly moved her to the middle of the street and as he pivoted to face the threat, he already had his short sword ready. However, he found he was standing face to face with a small figure wearing silk and covered with beautiful drapes.

Lidia stood with her maid servant gazing up at the young man, "I'm sorry, I didn't mean to frighten you," she said smiling. He was taken off guard but didn't lower his sword that was still pointed at her, so Merriam moved forward, grasped her friend's hand and turned to her escort, "She's my friend, it's all right."

He thought he had never seen such a beautiful face in all of his life, he swore she looked more like an angel than a person. Such beauty and grace! "Lady", he acknowledged and then simply stepped back and scanned the street searching for any other surprises. He would not be caught unaware again!

The girls stood close together and spoke urgently, "I don't have much time."

"Thank you Lidia, for coming; but I need to know. What has happened to Josheem? Doesn't he want to see me?"

"Please, you must not tell anyone, on your life!"

"Of course not but you must tell me. I had hoped to see him. . .but what is wrong? Something must be terribly wrong. Can I help?"

"No, no one can."

"You must tell me everything, please. You know how I feel about him."

"Merriam, I know you love him and he feels the same about you. Josheem is at home."

"At home? Then why didn't he present himself? I didn't even get to see him!"

"No, and you won't be able to see him again."

She heard what she was hoping never to hear and was still for a minute. Her heart was pounding; she took another breath, "Tell me Lidia. What is it? What has happened and why can't we meet?"

"This is it. Please tell no one! My family depends on it; he is at home; because he has leprosy."

Week 30

Secrets

L idia was in anguish and gripped both of Merriam's hands tightly, "Listen to me, you cannot tell anyone. Do you hear? You know what will happen to us if anyone should find out. The law says that he can't live at home anymore. He is unclean! Those that are stricken are banished to the caves for lepers. And their families are despised.

But my mother just couldn't let him go, he is sick! He needs to be cared for. So we made rooms for him in our stables at the edge of our pastures and my mother cooks for him and changes his bandages and he stays there.

We told everyone that he has gone to Jerusalem on business for the family and no one knows anything else. He is so sick, and I don't know what will happen to my mother and to all of us."

Everyone knew about leprosy—the disease that judged sinners and pronounced them unclean. Not only was there no treatment for the illness, but because it was a judgment by God, those who were afflicted were banished from their homes and shunned from the population. Often groups of the lepers would live at the edge of their village, they would help each other and their family members would sometimes go there and leave food and supplies. It was a terrible disease that always ended one way, in a very lonely death.

Lidia had to go back to her house before it was noticed that she was gone, so they embraced one more time, she looked fearfully into Merriam's face and nodded to her maid. Merriam continued to stand in the street, looking after her friend as she slipped back through the gate and then the minutes lengthened as she continued to stare. Finally her escort, returning his short sword to its sheath, made enough noise to get her attention, "Are you ready, ma'am?"

She nodded and numbly walked back to the side of the village where the household was staying. Her escort opened the gate to the walls that surrounded the beautiful inn and she went straight away to Deborah's suite.

Deborah was still being entertained; they had returned and were in the downstairs rooms. She was grateful for the time alone as she readied her lady's room for the night, then she stepped out onto the balcony. Voices from the lower rooms were clearer outside and she could hear Lord Balthazar and the other magi speaking to their host, explaining about the star they followed and the Newborn King they would meet.

Each seemed to have a special relationship with the star and what it meant to them. Their host kept them talking and discussing the Newborn long into the night. It wasn't often that the village entertained royalty and most never had the opportunity to see or speak to magi.

Tonight many of the village's citizens had heard about the amazing signs and wonders from the heavens; this would be talked about for a long time and would be the biggest event of their lives. She lingered on the balcony listening to the conversations and by the time the host had finished with his questions, she had a plan.

~~~~~~~~~~~~~~~~~~~~

Merriam was unusually quiet when Deborah returned back to her rooms; it had been a long day for them all. Priscilla gathered her garments and jewels for safekeeping and then left. Deborah was still awake when she said good night to Merriam as she left the room.

She was awake early and out of the house by herself, long before the household stirred. She walked to the other side of the village and waited secretly in the early morning darkness, watching the gates to her friend's household. She was draped in dark fabric from her head to her toes and was able to follow Lidia and her mother unseen when they emerged from their house with a large basket between them, headed for the edge of town.

She shivered, suddenly questioning her plan, "Am I crazy for doing this?" But she wasn't going to turn back now; she was determined.

The women stopped a short distance away from the stables. Then she saw a figure emerge from the dusk; she breathed softly to herself, "Is that him?"

No, it couldn't be, the figure had come nearer and she could tell it was an older man. In fact, he seemed to be very old and obviously a leper but still able to get around well. He went to the basket the women had put beside a rock but kept a distance away from them as they had a conversation that she couldn't hear.

She moved closer, hiding behind the outcrops of rocks. Once the man looked up, scanning the hillside and she froze. Did she make a sound that would betray her? She knew lepers were sometimes attacked by gangs from villages—she had heard of leper colonies being burned with everyone still in them. She knew they lived horrible lives, in fear of people and in fear and shame of their disease.

The conversation between the women and the man went on for several minutes, and once she could clearly hear a voice asking if there was enough water for the day. She also could hear the sounds of desperation and sorrow in the voices. At last they turned with bowed heads to leave, returning the way they had come.

Merriam was ready for this; she had moved through the rocks and scrub trees and was right behind the elderly man as he struggled to bring the basket through the stable opening.

However, she wasn't ready for the darkness and gloom that filled the interior. Soon she could see there were others inside in smaller makeshift rooms, she could see the struggling man with the basket ahead and she hurried to keep up. At first she was afraid someone would see her and call out an alarm, but she quickly observed that most were too sick to notice her and those that could still get up were helping those hopeless ones who couldn't move. And they were all terrible to look at.

She made the mistake of turning down the wrong hallway and stumbled when her feet struck a bundle on the floor. Steadying herself with a hand, she looked down, she cried out, "a baby!" Before she could stop herself, she crouched to lift the child back onto its makeshift bed. "Oh, thank you Jehovah! It is only a doll, a rag doll!" But in the next moment, tears were falling from her face when she realized that a doll meant that a child lived here, in these conditions. A child with leprosy!

Up ahead, the elderly man spoke a word and turned into a small doorway. And then she heard his voice! She kept close to the wall as she caught up and looked inside. She took a step closer.

She was standing in the entranceway when her eyes found him. He was helping the man lift the basket on a table. "I think you just like talking to the girls. It takes you longer and longer each time to return inside," he teased him.

He pushed his hand deep into the basket and rummaged around quickly, and then smiling at the older man, "Let me see here, I know my mother sent something that you might like, grandfather." He twisted back to find the "something special" and saw her.

They both froze. She stood still looking at him; his arm was deep in the basket, a smile still on his lips. The man saw her too and his eyes grew round and fearful, she could see now that the disease had claimed much of his face and his hands were both wrapped in dressings. And Josheem! There he stood on the remains of one leg.

She smiled. She was right to come here, she knew it.

She stepped into the room, holding out her hands, "Josheem! I have missed you so much."

He whirled back around behind the basket upon the table, "Merriam, you can't be here! What are you doing here?"

"No, I'm not here to run away. Listen to me. I know how to help you, to help you all," she said as she included them both in her smile. "There is someone who I am sure can and is willing to cure you. And I mean to take you to Him."

"You don't know what you are saying. Don't you see, don't you see me? We are all unclean, RUN! Get away while you can and pray that you don't get this living death. Please listen to me! I live an unclean life now; there is no hope, there is only agony. Don't you think my family would take care of me if it was possible?

I am outcast because God has found me guilty and judged me for my sin. Look on me and see the disease and the sores that are my sentence." He moved out from the side of the table, still away from her, with the obvious help of a crutch to show her the ravages of the disease on his body. She could also see the toll it had taken on his spirit.

"Now you must go, you have seen for yourself what I am and what is left of me." He gestured to the older man, "Please, grandfather will show you the way out because the stables are always dark. Now go."

The man hesitatingly looked up at her because it was obvious she wasn't moving, "No, I'm not going without you. You once said you love me, don't you remember?"

Josheem was in anguish, "How can you even mention that now? Don't you see what a filthy thing I really am?"

"I don't believe that, you are a good man. And I know that the One who can cure you is merciful and loving. Others may have, but He hasn't judged you."

"No, there is no hope. There is no one who is merciful and loving to a leper and please don't be so cruel as to make me believe in hope; because for me there is none. Just go, now I beg you. I have tried everything and even my family did as much as they could.

If you don't go soon, someone may see you and then you could be condemned as we are. Merriam, I love you too much to let any of this touch you."

"Josheem, I know what I'm doing. But now, I'll sit over here so you won't worry and I want to tell you about the Newborn and why I have faith He will cure you and everyone that comes to him. Just listen. Please trust me and then trust Him.

As you know, my lord Balthazar has been summoned by the Almighty God to welcome his Newborn Son. He has called my lord through prophecies and signs in the heavens and even by heavenly angels who have proclaimed His very birth. They have said that His Son will establish His kingdom here on earth and will bring all who worship Him to His everlasting kingdom.

My lord Balthazar and the other magi are obedient and are traveling to present themselves to the Newborn. However, instead of telling them where to find Him, Almighty God is perfecting their faith; He created a star that is guiding them, day by day and night by night. Josheem, the Newborn isn't just another king here on earth; He is much more powerful. You know my lord Balthazar, such a good man and he knows truth! He will bring your case before the King of kings, we have already seen miracles; the Newborn can and will cure you! Have faith in the One who is Lord of lords."

She stayed longer to talk and to ensure there was enough water and food for all and then tried to help those that needed bandage changes. Even though she had faith in the Newborn, she had found herself shrinking from the sores that she saw.

She found that the hopeless ones she helped actually helped her. They were patient with her as she tried to tie and then had to retie the bandages that slipped this way and that, never staying where she put them. Sometimes they laughed outright or looked away with a small smile as she wrestled the bandages to their places.

Hours had passed by the time Merriam left the stables exhausted. She carefully bathed outside the inn; scrubbing away any of the disease that lingered before she entered the household. She went to her room to change into a clean garment and then went to wait on her lady. Deborah was awake and was in the midst of listening to the head butler of the household complaining about the quality of the merchandise that he had been found in the village. She delicately lifted her eyebrows to acknowledge that she saw her as Merriam smoothed the silk chair covering, sat down and picked up her sewing basket.

Week 31

Following the Star Again

D eborah was finishing her morning household meetings. Since they expected to leave the village soon, she had made sure the supply lists were complete and then she oversaw the packing of provisions.

She turned to Merriam, "Did you sleep well last night?"

Merriam didn't look up from her work, but just the tone of the question caused her to flush, "My lady, I was up early this morning; certainly you don't think I was out all last night?"

As she finished her sentence, she looked up as she heard Deborah's laugh and felt her hand on her sleeve, "I'm teasing you. Really! I of all people know you are my best maid and a completely trustworthy and wonderful woman. But what is it? You are usually the one laughing and teasing me into a smile in the morning."

She was ready to tell her everything, that there was someone she loved that was seriously ill and she didn't know what to do except that she couldn't just leave him to the disease and hopelessness. She had actually opened her mouth when Lord Balthazar walked unannounced into the chamber. She immediately closed her mouth, rose, and curtsied.

He briefly inclined his head, "Ladies. Deborah, look! Even though it is still early in the day, our star is now outshining the sun! It is beautiful, can you believe it? Caspar is at his maps and thinks tonight we continue! Will everything be ready?"

"Yes my lord, everything will be ready, whenever you give us the message."

"Good! But I almost forgot! I have bought more of those beautiful horses to take home to our stables. The carts won't be ready for them until tomorrow; so we move out tonight, they will follow us as soon as they can in their own caravan. We may need to separate our household, but we are large enough to do that safely—they will catch up to us slowly."

Merriam couldn't believe what she was hearing; of course, this would work! If she could just get word to Josheem; he was a master equine handler and would be a wonderful help in moving the horses. If the trailing caravan was adding carts and handlers to their household, maybe this was the way to bring Josheem with them. She had faith that the Newborn would cure him.

He just needed to be hidden away from everyone during the day; it would be easier for him to be about during the night when they were moving and it was dark and shadowy. In fact, she was sure he would just be taken for another old man that was caring for the horses and then be left alone. The more she thought about it, the more she knew this was the right plan—surely they would find some way to get Josheem to the Newborn!

She longed to confide in Deborah but was just too afraid. Leprosy was not only a terrible disease, but most people believed it also indicated an evil person and was a curse from God. So she kept her thoughts and plans to herself.

Everyone was busy; the Royal Beacon could be seen shining even during the daytime and Balthazar had sent a message to Deborah that they had decided to leave as the sun went down. She had no doubts, she waited until after the noon hour when others were drowsy and had returned to their cots for their mid-day naps.

She took clothing, bandages, and drapes with her to the stables; and as she approached the entrance she was again struck by the gloom and hopelessness of those stricken with the disease. There were soft sounds of movement and occasional sighs. No voices were heard but only whispers or groans. Even in the stable, a place that was meant for animals, the lepers had to be careful that they weren't noticed. That would be dangerous; the world despised them and would have no compassion on them if they were found.

Merriam entered and drew back her veil in order to see better in the gloom, she moved forward uncertainly; it was so quiet. Where was everyone? She found Josheem's cot but he wasn't there and then finally heard quiet movement and murmurs nearby. She followed the sounds to a short corridor. Josheem was bending over the old man who was lying on a blanket on the floor,

"There. It's over now, you need to keep lying down for a while until you feel better." He turned around slowly as if he knew she was standing there.

"He was beaten by some of the village boys. He was one of our last links to the outside. We would send him for supplies, knowing he was one of the healthiest and that he still has family in the village. But no more."

"How bad is he?"

"He escaped, so he is not as bad as the villagers wanted him to be. But he was stuck by rocks, one of them hit the side of his infected shoulder; the skin just fell off so he bled badly at first. We are so happy that he made it back."

"Josheem, I have a plan and it will work."

Looking through the gloom Merriam could see the anger in Josheem's eyes, "Nothing will help us, and we are condemned! You just don't see," raising both arms to include everyone there, "we are all dead."

Merriam shook her head and raised her voice so all could hear, "No, that is what I am telling you. Hope has come! You don't see the sky in here, but the beacon is there, the light that the magi are following. A Divine King will be born, my lord Balthazar, and the magi lords have been summoned to Him. They know Him or believe enough to search for Him to learn if He is the One. Think! This King is the King spoken of by the prophets; He can cure you. And I know he will."

Josheem countered, "Why do you think the newborn King of kings will think any differently than the rest of His people? Why don't you think He will not just execute us? We are hated. We could never even approach the lowliest of His kingdom."

"You can because my lord Balthazar has been told that He calls everyone to Himself and that He has been born to establish His Kingdom and will rule forever. His kingdom will be for all that come to Him. He is powerful and compassionate; He will cure you."

"Would He cure me?" grandfather asked. He was still hurting but he had wrapped his blanket around himself and; struggling to sit up, looked at her with hope.

She nodded, "He will."

Josheem stared at her for a long while and then asked quietly, "You have a plan?"

The caravan started out of the village following the Royal Star as the sun dipped below the horizon; the supply train was noticeably bigger. There were more people serving the households now and everyone was busy. It was good to be back and moving in the caravan; everyone's job was important.

The second caravan prepared to leave the village the next night. It was equipped just as carefully as the first household, but smaller and it would carry Balthazar's newly-purchased prize horses and their special keepers. There were new grooms in addition to the ones that had traveled with them from home, and a new Master Equine Handler that would ensure the new horses' safety. These beautiful animals were known for their strength and courage, but also for their tempers so they were given special carts, grooms and handlers that knew how to keep them happy. They were important and valuable signs of the royal class enjoyed by their master.

The next evening came and as the night became darker the following caravan slowly left the village. The household staff had its own work and mostly left the handlers alone to care for the temperamental beauties so it appeared as though there were two households in the one caravan. The household staff noticed the handlers saying tearful goodbye to their families while oddly keeping a distance from them and assumed this was because they didn't want strangers coming close and agitating the horses. Then everyone went about their jobs as both caravans followed the glorious star.

Week 32

The Truth and the Way

C aspar leaned over to Balthazar and clasped his arm, saying "Beautiful, isn't it? The top edge of the star seems to touch heaven and the tail sits on the earth as though Almighty God is saying he has created the way for us to come to Him."

Caspar's words seemed to echo in Balthazar's mind and they both heard the voice that they recognized as that of the Newborn King,

> *"I am the truth and the way. None can come to the Father except through me."*

"The truth and the way." Both men looked toward each other in the night, aware that these words and their thoughts had come from the Newborn.

~~~~~~~~~~~~~~~~~~~~

The caravans were still miles apart from each other, but kept in constant communication through a series of riders. Both households were experienced caravan travelers, but this was different. They all shared the feeling that they were on an adventure that was becoming more and more exciting. They were now a very large group, and they were led by three royal

170

magi who had obviously been summoned by the heavens. No one knew where these travels would lead, but they were all willing to follow the light.

Week 33

Sandstorm!

The caravans continued toward the west for several nights. A routine began of waking as the sun was setting, and traveling through the cool darkness of the night following the Royal Star.

Merriam made sure there was a note for Josheem with the riders that rode between the caravans each night. Several of her friends knew she was sending messages to someone special and teased her about him. They knew he was one of the equestrian handlers but had never seen him. This wasn't odd because there were miles between the caravans but they were sure they would meet him when they reached their destination and the camps would link again.

So until they actually met him, they could make up all kinds of things about him. She enjoyed their teasing and they made her forget about the disease that Josheem carried. She became stronger in her belief and finally truly knew that the Newborn was their hope.

Josheem found the daily routine pleasant and he felt safer than he had in a long time. Without the constant need to be alert for ambushes from villagers, he was able to care for the horses entrusted to him and he enjoyed the work. Grandfather had come with him but he mostly stayed in the cart since he was very weak, venturing out only occasionally.

~~~~~~~~~~~~~~~~~~~~

Desert travel was always dangerous and one of the many reasons was because of the weather. The miles and miles of sand and hills dissected by old worn caravan paths were alternately baked during the day by a full sun that could register somewhere about 130 degrees and then frozen at the night during the winter. Sandstorms were common and could surprise the most experienced travelers by seeming to appear out of nowhere with tragic results. The sand carried on 100 mph winds could literally beat caravans to death.

The caravan master and the magi knew about these dangers and took precautions by always being on the lookout for cues that the weather was changing. There were contingencies for overheating, freezing, dry oases, and sandstorms because these plans saved lives.

So far they had encountered nothing unusual and the weather was what their guides had expected. Unfortunately, as the caravans were starting to make camp for the approaching day, it became obvious that a sandstorm was likely. Even before the sun reached the horizon, the temperature was hotter than usual. Puffs of air lifted the edges of tarps off of bundles and a spreading gray cloud could be seen in the distance, as it got lighter. The caravans had almost closed the gap and stopped with just one hill between them. Each was making camp to rest for the day; this time however, everyone was on edge.

The magi were conferring with one of the guides, "I agree, I don't believe the wind will miss us, is everything secure?" asked Balthazar.

"Yes your majesty, but I am hoping the brunt of the storm will miss us since we have camped in a bowl between the hills," he replied. "Unless you suggest we change locations?"

"No, I think you have found the best camp for us. I am afraid we will have to weather this one."

"Thank you majesty." The guide turned back to tell his aides to pass the word that this was indeed the campsite and today they would need to double rope.

Balthazar looked back toward the west. He couldn't see the second caravan because it was sitting low in the bowl behind the last hill. He again felt the heat seem to rise. He looked to Illya, "Can you feel the change in the air? Plan for a bad storm and send word to the following caravan to stay where they are until I say otherwise."

"I'll send one last rider on his way. My lord, do you have any special instructions for the handlers of your horses?"

"Yes. Do anything it takes to keep them safe. They will know what to do."

"Of course, my lord."

Instead of the household drowsily making camp and drifting off to sleep as the day and heat began, there was a scurry of activity and then a sort of a tense waiting. Some paced and kept watch as the wind started to gust, others tried to sleep. Merriam had a note ready for the rider to take back to Josheem and had placed it in his bag seconds before he was off to the second caravan.

Living in the desert, Josheem had witnessed many sandstorms before and he knew early on that they would not be able to avoid this one. It could easily be seen on the horizon and it was getting bigger and stronger as it steered closer.

He was worried. He had cared for horses all of his life and he knew the Arabians were high-strung and skittish. They were extremely sensitive and intelligent but they would easily injure and kill themselves as they tried to escape from something they didn't understand. As their caravan stopped and the carts were being settled, the horses were already aware of something "wrong" in the air. Their eyes had grown wide, their sensitive nostrils twitched and they nervously stomped their hooves as they finally allowed themselves to be led from the cart to the makeshift stalls that were rebuilt each day for them to rest in.

Josheem instructed each of the handlers to stay with their horse during the storm; he didn't want any to get loose. They groomed and fed the horses their special diet and Josheem added some herbs that he had used before to help calm and relax them.

Each of the horses were then placed in the special coats they wore in the daytime, designed to keep the sun off of them, but instead of resting in their stalls alone, the handlers were nearby, sitting at the stall gate. Each one wore a personalized halter and each of the handlers had another bridle ready and a silken mask in case they needed to contain a panicking horse.

Josheem had kept his distance from the other workers as he gave orders, and then relied on an assistant to follow up and answer any questions. The handlers didn't pay any attention to this behavior; Josheem knew horses and they were glad to work with someone so knowledgeable. At the end of the journey when they got the horses safely home to Balthazar's palace, they knew they would receive a large bonus. Their lord was known for his generosity and honesty.

A rider from the main caravan approached the smaller camp; the lookouts had already announced him. He first spoke to the steward and gave him the bag of instructions he carried. He then found the horses and their handlers. He loved looking at these beautiful creatures, their eyes were large and seemed to talk to him, their manes flowed like rivers from their necks and their legs tapered to hoofs that shone.

They were the smartest animals he had ever known, smarter than most people he had met. He grew concerned about the approaching storm when he saw how they stomped and twitched their necks, causing their manes to fly about their bodies.

He came near to one of the beauties and greeted his friend who was its handler, "Greetings to you, Zoab, how is your beautiful one here? She looks anxious."

Zoab was grooming the mare in long comforting strokes, "She is smart. She doesn't like the weather and knows it will get worse. She is telling me about it. I think she holds it against me!" Both men chuckled quietly, not wanting to disturb any of the horses.

The rider stayed to watch Zoab groom the horse and then arrange her special coat over her gleaming back. He then asked for Josheem and was told that he was as usual somewhere in the stables. The rider had the note in his hand and began to walk among the stalls, noticing the handlers at each horse's side.

He found Josheem inspecting a hoof at the far end of the stable, it was shadowy and dark and again the rider was amazed that the man worked so hard and even placed himself in position of a lower worker. Usually a man with this much authority and responsibility would have been at the front of the stables, in the light; but Josheem cared so much for the horses and the handlers that he worked hard and placed himself where others didn't want to be.

The noise outside seemed to change and the rider had to shout to be heard when he found Josheem and then saw him start at his voice, "Here's another note for you!"

Josheem glanced up at the rider but then his eyes widened at something over his shoulder and he shouted, "Down! Now!"

Week 34

Sandblasted

A sound like cannon fire blasted into the stable right before massive gusts of wind rammed into the stable crushing wooden beams and posts into slivers, and sending everything else flying. Screams of people and animals could be heard between the thunderous gusts of wind. The handlers were fighting to grab the harnesses in between the wind gusts, in order to contain the horses.

"Forget the harnesses, take cover!" yelled Josheem.

People were no longer trying to hold on to possessions, they were trying to stay alive in the swirling gusts that threw them in the air and blasted them with sand. Through all of this, each of the horses were surrounded by several handlers and somehow masked, even though the stronger harnesses had been lost. The men struggled to keep them calm as they desperately bucked and reared to try to run from this fearful thing.

A cart that held food turned up on its end, and full water casks fell down into the driver's seat, knocking the man unconscious. The camels simply lay down and lowered their huge eyelashes securely over their eyes. The midday sun was blocked out by the blowing sand, so it was dark as night but the temperature was still scorching.

People ran back and forth, screaming in pain as they tried to find cover from the hot, blasting sand that struck at them.

The messenger was still trying to find cover, his arms over his head. He heard a nearby shout, "Watch out!" and then the crack of disintegrating wood just before he felt a terrific hit to the head and then his world went black.

As the smaller caravan was being hit by the sandstorm, the larger one was quiet. They knew what was happening because of the huge sand cloud that had moved over the hill and sat squarely on the camp.

Madai paced in front of the rider. He would be reporting to his lord in a few moments and would say that he wouldn't send another rider back to the small camp right now. He wanted to wait until he thought the rider could make it through the wind and pummeling sand. The earlier courier hadn't returned, of course; the sandstorm had arrived while he was back at the smaller camp and it was worse than they had thought it would be. No one was surprised that he hadn't returned, but they should have received some word by this time. So they had to wait.

As evening approached, the wind gusts finally started slowing down and there was still no word. Balthazar came to believe the second caravan needed help. He decided not to wait any longer and sent food and water with a large rescue group back to them. "Send back a rider with a report as soon as you get there!"

Night came and the star stood still. The magi gathered in their tent to talk about their situation and to plan.

Week 35

Found Out

T he rescue group from the large caravan made slow progress; even though the giant Royal Star stood like a huge
sentry in the sky, the night was black. Daniel, the lead rider
was straining to see any camp lights that would lead them to
the small caravan. "I can't see anything and I know we are
approaching where they were camped. No lights. No sounds.
Where are they?"

He got down from his horse and stood completely still,
"What is it, Daniel?" asked his friend.

"I may have heard something, some small sound. But it is
gone now."

"Wait! Here, the camp is. . .or was here!" Daniel had
moved over to check some shadows nearby and then saw
the wreckage. He could see it then. Just ahead the caravan
was in shambles, no structure was left standing—tents were
gone, the carts and containers had been smashed and the
less wounded were tending the more wounded.

All the horses were gone, no one knew if they had escaped
the devastating storm or if they lay wounded or dead in
the desert.

Those in security were attempting to create a perimeter,
and were gathering all the wounded and dead inside a safe
area. They knew bandits roamed the desert freely, and would
certainly attack the camp if they were found in this condition.

And with all of the bleeding injured, predators would quickly appear that fed on the wounded and dead, and cleaned the desert of messes such as this.

There was no way and no one to go for help, they were depending on the larger caravan to recognize what had happened and send aid before either predator found them.

~~~~~~~~~~~~~~~~~~~~

"Josheem!" He heard the soft call again but he couldn't see where it came from. Did he dare to come out of hiding, to help one of those who would hate him when they saw his disease?

"Where are you? I can't see you," he reluctantly called back. Josheem felt overwhelmed by the need to help a fellow sufferer so he drew away from the side of the hill that he had gone in order to stay away from the others.

Ironically, this hill kept him safer than most of the others during that horrible storm. He had been struck by flying pieces of wood from the stables, but he had wrapped clean cloths around those wounds. The leprosy had cut off much of the blood supply to his limbs, so he didn't bleed as much as a healthy man would have. So now, he even kind of looked like one of the wounded helping others.

Even though it was dark, Josheem pulled his cloak further over his face and headed out for the first time in over a year to go out among those without the disease. He walked toward the place where he thought he had last heard the voice and immediately was caught in the chaos.

Bleeding and injured, dying and dead people seemed to be scattered everywhere and most seemed to have stayed where they had been thrown by the wind. A young man had a piece of the timber from a food cask impaled in his leg, he was on the ground, crying out in pain and two older men were at his side. Several water kegs had been tossed on the very top of the tent cart. Not a drop had been spilled. People were scurrying everywhere; calling out to others and cries were heard above the soft groans.

And then he heard him again, "Josheem." He turned to search the other side of the camp wondering how could he hear this soft voice from so far away? It didn't make sense.

He was walking toward the call when a man grabbed his elbow, "Please help me, please!" Josheem jumped at the contact. He had not been touched by anyone in such a long time; the simple act stopped him in his tracks.

It was a frightened young man and he begged, "My wife, she is hurt and I can't pick her up, please help us!" and as he said this, the man grasped Josheem's arm again.

Josheem was frightened. . .by everything. He wanted to help this man but he also knew he had to answer the person who was calling to him. Whose voice could that be?

Even though it was dark and people were dying, he had to be careful. He had seen what people do when they are confronted with those who have leprosy. Bad things happen to lepers who don't run away before healthy people get close; he had seen that many times and there was no mercy. But this man desperately needed his help, but Josheem dare not get close or be seen by anyone. He would be smart to just run away.

The young man was surprisingly strong, however; he turned to a small woman on the ground, "Shhhh; here is a strong man that will help us now. Don't worry, dearest one."

He couldn't turn away now. Josheem could see through the gloom the outline of a young woman, just about the age of his sister, who looked like she had been hit with something from behind. Her headdress was off and blood was oozing from a long gash that seemed to run from ear to ear at the back of her head.

Josheem sat down close by and looked at her, "Let's not move her right now. I can help. He took some of his linens of the type that he frequently used for himself, from a deep satchel he carried on his shoulder.

Speaking comforting words that he frequently used when he helped other lepers, he said, "Sister, please let me look at your wound; I will not hurt you." And with that, Josheem no longer thought of himself as he tenderly cared for her until it was safe to hold the dressings secure as her husband carried her to a cot under the medical tent. As he helped place her gently on the cot, he turned quickly to leave and then felt a hand stop him.

He had not been fast enough, he heard her sharp intake of breath but her hand was still gently on his arm. He kept his face away, even though it was dark, and waited for the scream and the scrambling of bodies away from him.

Her hand came to rest up higher on his shoulder, "Bless you my friend. Bless you."

Josheem was stunned, "You're welcome sister. You will feel better very soon; now I must go." He ducked his head but he knew she had seen him. Was she too injured to believe her eyes? He quickly navigated to the other side of the camp, listening for the voice that was calling him.

A miracle! He heard it again, but he could only see a pile of poles and wooden beams. Could this be what was left of the stables?

Again he heard it, he drew closer and moved some piles of hay; and then there was another person at his side, "I think I hear voices in here. I think I saw some women and some of the children go into the stable just before the strongest wind hit. The young man then turned to others and raised his voice, "We need help over here! Everyone!"

Josh was too frightened to turn around and run, several other men were immediately there and started moving poles and planks. "Josheem, help," the voice came again but this time it was weaker. He picked up the nearest pole and pushed it away, and waded into the mess. He straightened his shoulders thinking, "If I am going to be found out and taunted, then I will be found out and taunted for the human being that I am, not a coward."

"Here, here they are!" He saw arms and legs but virtually nothing else; but they were moving! The men rushed over to him and frantically began to work the debris away.

During the storm the young rider who was the messenger had quickly made a safe area for the children that had come to the stable for shelter, several of the children were packed tightly in a corner and even though they were sandblasted and windblown, they were virtually unhurt.

However, his legs had been shattered by the wood beams when they fell, and he was not moving. He had been pushed, sitting up, tightly into what was left of the wall. His eyes moved to Josheem's face.

"Josheem, I knew you could do it, I know you because your lady tells all who will listen what a good man you are," he whispered. Josheem forgot himself—he forgot all of the hurt and anger he had known since it was discovered he had leprosy. He even forgot that he had been driven from his home and village by his so-called friends and neighbors. He didn't even remember that he was outcast and unclean.

The man's arms lay still, his chest only slightly moving. Josheem removed the linens he had gathered around himself in order to hide his disease and using the skills he had learned in the leper colony, he bound the man's legs snuggly in order to stop the bleeding, splint the broken bones, and hopefully, hold off shock.

Josheem picked up the remnant of a door. "You need to trust me. I am going to use this as a cot to move you away from the wall and to let you lie down. If you don't lie down, I can't stop the bleeding and you will soon die."

The man just nodded and grasped his hand tightly for an instant, then lost consciousness as he started to roll him to the side to move him.

Josheem desperately looked around for help, he prayed, "Oh Lord, I know you have rightly judged those of us who are unclean. But I ask that you hear my prayer, the prayer of an unworthy man and a judged sinner, please help me to help this one, who is your servant." Several of the men who tended the food supplies were close by, they had a cart that they had put together again after the storm and were searching for the scattered supplies and utensils.

He called to them, "Here, over here. I need help with this man, he is severely injured." They immediately picked through the debris to get to them, and then followed Josheem's directions on how to maneuver the man onto the cart. As they worked, they turned back to him, "Where do you want us to take him?"

"Over to the large tent, he needs more care." And they all worked together to leverage the man onto the cot and get him out of the stable area without much more blood loss. Josheem held the crushed leg in place so the bleeding wouldn't begin again. They arrived at the tent and as they lay the man down, one of those helping him looked over at Josheem to ask him about the man, and it happened.

"Leprosy! This man is a leper!" he screamed at the top of his lungs.

The medical assistant who had been holding the injured man's other leg threw it down as he stepped backwards as fast as he could. "Evil, that's what has happened, there is evil here!" as he turned his face away.

The tent and the entire small caravan were again in an uproar, this time it was against Josheem. "Get away from us! GO!"

Josheem had heard all of this before, he had hastily caught the injured man's leg as it fell and he placed it gently on the cot. When he looked up, everyone had backed up from him, leaving a growing circle. He hunched his shoulders; he needed to run away somewhere, before the rocks began to be thrown.

"Unclean! You don't belong here, get away!" The shouts were rapidly getting louder and fear was rapidly turning into hate. Some of the men had picked up some of the wooden posts and lifted them menacingly. The caravan had now found an outlet for their fear and anger over the storm.

Man of God

𑁋

"If you send him away, you will be losing the master horseman and you are wrong. He is a good worker and a good man," the voice was from one with authority. The crowd had been getting louder but were distracted when they heard the voice and turned back to look at the man.

His voice rose again, "You call him unclean; however, we know we are all unclean in the eyes of Almighty God. Only through His mercy are we spared." The voice was one of power and it came from an old man with a staff that was accompanied by another man.

Pointing at the rider with the shattered leg, he said "Now, help this man, he is need of help and he is close to dying right in front of you."

Those that had been in the middle of shouting seemed to do exactly what the man told them to do. They returned to the patient and started to work. The others in the caravan eyed them all from a safe distance.

Josheem had been ready to run, and now he couldn't believe what he was hearing! There was someone who saw him not as an evil thing to destroy, but as a person. He stood very still with his head down.

The stranger looked at him for a long minute. "You haven't had the disease for very long, have you? But why did you put yourself in the position to be found out by others?" asked the older man, while the younger one stood by closely.

Josheem was still wondering if he could run, "I know I shouldn't have been here, but this man was injured and I couldn't just leave him. You're right, I've haven't had the disease for long, but since I had to live in the leper colony, I have gained a lot of medical knowledge. I frequently help others who are much worse off than me so I knew what to do and I couldn't just let him die."

"You knew that those you were helping would certainly pay you back by trying to harm you. Serving those unselfishly who have threatened you and certainly won't thank you, you are a blessing from God." As the older man was speaking, he looked at the younger one frequently as if he were teaching him. "My name is Simeon, and my friend and I are glad to meet you."

Josheem raised his face, knowing Simeon would see his mutilated skin; but for once in a long time, he was unafraid. "My lord, I am Josheem, Master Equine Handler for my lord Balthazar and I am thankful for your presence and I thank you for your concern for me. I'm sorry, I don't know you, but you and your companion have saved me from an angry crowd."

Week 37

Simeon

❧

"Josheem, you are welcome. I live in the temple in Jerusalem, and I am just returning home after a short journey. My companion wanted to find the caravan of the magi. This is my companion–"

"Shadrach, my friend!" spoke Balthazar as strode through the shambles around him to place his hand on the companion's shoulder.

Few had noticed Balthazar and the small group as they rode into the caravan with supplies, and even fewer noticed when Balthazar breathed a prayer of thanksgiving when he saw Shadrach.

"My lord" replied Shadrach and had sunk to his knees before Balthazar raised him and clasped him; both men, wept with joy at their reunion. No one could hear their confidences as they spoke to each other.

In a minute Balthazar looked at Simeon, "Welcome to my caravan, our hospitality may be thin, but not because of lack of reverence for a man of God, especially the man of God who saved my friend."

"King Balthazar, thank you for your welcome. I know of you and I know of your journey to welcome the Newborn King of kings. I am praying for you. You seek God and I know you have sought His mercy for your friend. You honor Almighty God with your humble spirit."

"Even though we weren't affected by the storm, we seem to have been led here to help. One of your workers needs attention and we may be able to assist."

"Thank you for your kindness. We have been severely challenged by this storm." Those who were still gathered around heard him continue quietly, "I have come to know that the best equine handler that works for me has been found to have leprosy. I confess I do not know what to do."

"Will you forgive him?

"What?"

"Can you forgive him? Can you see that the disease is an illness and not a judgment from God? Forgive him just as you certainly forgave this man that killed another?"

This was a new concept; even those who were educated often had cruel ideas about the disease of leprosy. There were so many tales surrounding the disease and the afflicted ones that it was difficult to know what was truth and what was simply hate.

An hour later Balthazar and Simeon were in deep discussion in front of the tent where the injured were being treated. The work had been going on around them. As they talked, Balthazar had the feeling that these words were like drops of mercy and knowledge straight from heaven. He listened carefully and learned.

They talked about judgment, mercy, truth, and, then about the Son of the Most High. Balthazar learned that Simeon had been told by God that he would live to see His Son, the Royal Newborn. So, Simeon lived at the temple in Jerusalem, praying night and day, waiting for the Promise.

Balthazar also learned that in obedience, Simeon had journeyed from the temple on a mission to gather Shadrach as his assistant. He also knew from the vision that there would be a time when they would be sent to intercept a caravan.

"Yes, I can forgive him; and yes, I do forgive him," answered Balthazar. And as he said that, the star that had been very still in the sky gave a great flash of brilliant light and seemed to be gathering itself to move again.

"Then after we help here, we will be on our way. I don't think we will meet again, King Balthazar. I know the Royal Son will arrive soon, and I have been promised that I will see him." He then smiled, "Then I hope to depart this earth for a much better place."

The men arose and followed Simeon as he went to look in on the wounded in the tent. He was still smiling as they gasped, there seemed to be a great change in everyone. The man with the shattered legs sat up and swung both healthy legs to the ground and walked easily. There were gasps of delight and prayers lifted up.

The glow from the mighty star lit the sky and the sandy desert, Josheem could clearly be seen, healthy. Everyone had been healed! A miracle had happened in the midst of a disaster; and the Royal Newborn was calling them.

The Royal Star

Shouts of joy came from those nearby, there was a sudden rush as several standing nearby ran off to tell others and then everyone that was left crowded close. This was an amazing miracle and of course it was a miracle because these things just don't happen. Who was this Royal Son of the Most High that the old man spoke about, the King of kings that even cared about a leper? Maybe He would be a King for all of them.

Balthazar was overwhelmed as he watched his friend leave with the man of God. He felt tears running down his face and he whispered his question, "Are you truly God? And if so, what would you have me do now, Royal Son?" In response, the great star visibly began moving.

By now the larger caravan had sent riders and more carts. The small caravan had been restored, supplies had arrived from the larger one and they were mobile, again. They found that there had been so much damage that they would just reform into one caravan.

"We move, we move now and follow our star!" shouted Balthazar. He hadn't needed to shout; everyone was watching the skies and knew what to do.

Balthazar stayed with the smaller caravan as it traveled to the larger one and then the two combined. He was happier than he had been in a long time and urged everyone forward. They were following the Royal Star and it was moving toward Jerusalem!

At Herod's Palace

𝒮𝓇

The magi were preparing to ride into Jerusalem and were being accompanied by a large retinue of servants and soldiers. They were leaving the caravan encamped outside the city with the orders to be ready to move as soon as they returned. They had continued to discuss how they would approach King Herod and to assess the most up to date news from their informants inside the palace.

They were used to royal intrigue and knew information was key to their purpose and their safety. They wanted to find out everything Herod had been told or knew about the Newborn's birth and they wanted to see for themselves if the stories they had heard about Herod were true. Was he was degenerating into a monster who frequently murdered to get what he wanted?

Their informants told stories of mass murders and even whispered that the heir, the eldest royal son, had not been seen in a while and no one seemed to know where he had gone. Previously he had always accompanied his father and now he wasn't mentioned at all and no one dared ask. Madai brought a message to Balthazar that he had received from an informant.

He read, "It is getting much worse. Everyone knows of someone who has been accused of something, anything, and then just disappears. All it takes is for Herod to take a disliking to anyone and then they will soon be dead. There is even talk that Herod becomes enraged and murders innocent people in front of the royal court in the throne room. I wouldn't normally have believed that but I have seen great pools of dried blood on the floor."

The magi were waiting in an adjoining room. They had sent greetings to King Herod and his court, identified themselves, and asked to enter his kingdom. There had been the usual royal reply and an additional note saying they would enjoy the opportunity to meet with the magi.

Melchior had visited Jerusalem just before Herod was King and often spoke of the great Jewish Temple and the knowledge that was stored in the libraries of King Solomon. The history of the prophets, their prophecies, and the life of their King David, were well documented. He had found that the libraries had been turned into storage sheds and the books had all been destroyed.

~~~~~~~~~~~~~~~~~~~~

They were now preparing to enter the throne room to greet Herod, who, they were told, was anxiously waiting to welcome them. They didn't come as supplicants–they were royalty from extremely powerful families and they were magi. He would be foolish to ignore them and possibly offend them as they traveled across his land.

Illya finished smoothing the pleats on Balthazar's robe and then set about directing the other wardrobe servants to ensure their king looked his best. He was frightened for them all; he had heard many stories about Herod's cruelty and was especially frightened by the details of what could only be called madness.

He could only pray that Herod would see his Lord Balthazar as an imposing royal mage from a family that controlled most of the known world and then be able to restrain himself from doing harm to any of them. However, he had heard that he rarely deigned to control himself.

Herod was made king of Jerusalem by Rome and he was supposed to do whatever it took to ensure the Jews behaved. Herod liked doing whatever he wanted to do and he had found that he liked violence. He had discovered that killing the innocent usually led to getting what he wanted. He had found a powerful tool, and one he enjoyed.

Balthazar held absolutely still as Illya seated his crown, layering it on top of the silken tapestry that had first been laid across his head. The tapestry had been woven by Priscilla to give the effect of gold when you saw it from one angle and then it would change to silver when it was observed from another angle. It was beautiful and a perfect setting for the ancient royal crown he wore as King and sole ruler of Arabia and all its lands.

Illya's hands were shaking and he couldn't get the crown seated and started to try again when Balthazar reached up and took it from his hands. He looked intently at him with a very calm gaze. "Illya, listen to me. All will be well. You will be fine. It is important to me that you complete my wardrobe so I can join the others. The sooner I am able to do that, the sooner we will be able to leave here."

Illya flushed with embarrassment. "Yes, of course my lord."

The magi had contacts in the palace that were paid very well to keep their ears open and to report back to them about what Herod was doing and saying. Frighteningly, some of these trusted contacts had recently disappeared. The magi knew that under most circumstances, even Herod would not try to harm or delay them, but the information they had been getting about him was that he was so evil they could only believe he was mentally unstable.

They knew he had questioned every prophet and magician in his kingdom about the Newborn, and tortured those that he thought knew more than they were telling, in order to plan how he might find and destroy Him.

Herod had lived a lifetime killing those who stood in his way and he was ready to make sure this Newborn would not get in his way.

Now he desperately wanted to know everything they knew about this King that they were searching for. Before they would tell him what they knew of the Newborn, they needed to know if he knew anything at all about where He was.

They had planned their conversations well and had arranged cues for each other. He must have some information from his seers or prophets; obviously it wasn't enough to alert him but it may help them. They did know that he wasn't searching on his own for the Newborn and they couldn't understand why.

They spoke quietly. Caspar looked at Melchior and Balthazar, "I agree, he will do what it takes to find out what we know. Our informant has told me that he has placed a new person in our household, someone close to us, to get information to him."

Melchior sighed. This was not the court that it was when he had visited here before. Instead of a gathering of minds to search for truth and answers, there was only hate and fear now. "I have the worst possible feeling about him and our interview with him. He is evil, I tell you. Have you heard from any of our people here in the palace who the informant is?"

"Yes and it was very unimaginative of Herod. He unfortunately asked our own informant on him to be his spy. I am glad to know that we can control some of the information that he is hearing. The rest of our people in the palace are terrified of him, as you can imagine. They describe the horrible things he does and the evil he is planning; most of it I just can't believe."

Balthazar joined them in the opulent room after he was fully dressed by Illya, "Let's be genial while keeping our eyes and ears open; but don't eat or drink anything! My latest information is that Herod has become interested in poison and many people have succumbed. Now, I want to accomplish this as quickly as possible so I can leave and bathe. I am feeling dirty."

He finished his sentence just as the royal pages arrived in the room to escort them to Herod's throne room.

~~~~~~~~~~~~~~~~~~~~

They looked at each other, affirming their agreement and left to walk into the throne room that seemed to be miles long. However, they were royalty also, from centuries-old powerful ruling families and they looked it. They were magi and known to have almost magical powers that were beyond most others imagination. They were educated and politically connected, their countries would never be threatened by Rome so they were not afraid of Herod and he knew it.

They were in slow procession, arrayed in silks and fabrics beyond compare; their jewels were of the size and type that made Herod gasp with envy. They were accompanied by attendants dressed as beautifully as most royals.

They halted just short of the steps up to the throne and Herod did not stand to greet them. They remained standing as their entourage continued to adjust and move, but the magi were completely still. There was a crowd of attendants positioned on the dais and many others were gathered in the room to see the revered magi. The crier continued announcing them, calling out their names, their positions and their authorities—gratifyingly it went on and on.

Herod sat on his throne, impressed and jealous. When he was jealous, he was dangerous. He had wanted the magi within his palace so he could control them and find out what he wanted to know about the Newborn from them. His plans had all failed, he moved his fingers on his right hand and his chief magician was at his elbow.

"They look fabulously rich, are we getting tribute from them? I want their jewels."

"Your majesty, these men are not simply kings. They are foreigners from lands that are friends of Rome, and they are magi. They are not in our jurisdiction; they are honored, royal guests."

"No! I am king and my word is law. And I tell you I mean to make them pay—look at their jewels, have you ever seen jewels that size?"

"Majesty, what would you have me to do?"

"I want to ask them some questions, I want to catch them in a lie, or something so I can accuse them of enough to detain them. You make it happen."

The chief of Herod's advisors was at his other elbow, speaking quietly and urgently, "Majesty, please resist that idea. These men have large armies and powerful lands; and they are backed by Rome. Rome would not be happy."

Rudely, Herod was still seated and conferring with his advisors as the magi continued to wait. "Oh, it always comes to that, to what Rome wants. Well, we will see."

Herod sat with his eyes half closed for a short time more, then he seemed to rouse himself. Standing slowly he pasted a frightening-looking smile on his face, "Welcome royal friends; welcome to our kingdom and our palace. To what do we owe the pleasure of your company?"

Balthazar had been completely still. He had been praying that this would be a safe and quick interview. He had looked at the Royal Star through open windows before he had been escorted into the throne room and he gained confidence when it seemed to be undisturbed.

He didn't bow or even dip his head, but raised his hand to encompass the others and began, "Herod, we are honored to be in your presence. Please accept our greetings and wishes for your health. We are on pilgrimage and must cross your kingdom. We come to pay our respects to you, great king, and to ask permission for our caravan to traverse your kingdom."

Herod's beady eyes never left Balthazar's face, his right hand clinched and unclenched. He looked like a snake readying to strike. "Pilgrimage? Oh, and we had so hoped you would be able to stay and take your leisure here in Jerusalem with us."

"We welcome the invitation, and would normally accept your offer but according to our custom; we cannot tarry on our journey. We must not turn aside from our promise to travel to greet the Newborn King.

We have been told of his pending birth. We ask your majesty; however, where has the Newborn King been born? Where is He? We seek Him."

Herod continued to stare at the magi as he moved his hand and uttered to his right, "Morden, where in *my* kingdom is this so called new king? When was or where will He be born, just *where*?" Herod's voice had been rising and it cracked loudly at the end of his last question. The entire throne room was quiet.

The older man pitifully came forward bowing, "Majesty, we have read of His coming, and the prophets all say He has been born and is with His family now. Just where, we are unsure." The magician's voice had dropped with each thing he reported. Now he looked beseechingly at the others for help.

"Unsure, you mean you don't have an answer for me?" Herod's voice was ominously quiet; there was not another sound in the entire room. Then his hands rolled into fists and his face started twitching.

Morden tried to sound calm but couldn't, "N-n-n-n-no, Majesty; it seems as though some of the prophets have said Jerusalem but it is more than likely another town much smaller. But there are no royal families left outside of Jerusalem after you k-k-k-k; I mean to say, there are no royal families except your; uh, you my king."

Not looking at him, Herod continued in his quiet voice, "Enough! So you don't know and you are my chief magician!" Then Herod simply glanced again at his magician and he was taken from the room by guards.

The magi stood and watched in amazement during this time, they wanted to look at each other to gauge what each one thought, but didn't want to give anything away.

"Enough," thought Balthazar. Briskly he continued so all could hear, "King Herod, we don't know where He is either. No one knows, but we still travel. Thank you, your majesty; we must be on our way." Balthazar knew this was the time to sweep out and ultimately get away; the stench of death was too strong here.

Herod was taken unaware with Balthazar's boldness and was briefly unsure about what to do. He dared not stop them; even he had to acknowledge the mighty influence and powers that magi had at their disposal. He said nothing then a quiet silky voice rose from Herod as the magi were preparing to leave, "Farewell. Oh, when you find Him, let me know. I want to. . .worship. . .Him, also."

A brisk nod, "of course," and the three magi turned their backs to Herod and left the throne room.

Week 40

Leaving Jerusalem

❦

"All is ready, your highness," reported Madai as the magi marched down the long staircase outside of the throne room. They showed no sign of slowing down.

Balthazar fixed him with a knowing look, "Watch our backs; I believe we will need extra security."

He nodded in understanding, "It has already been done, Sire." He then lowered his voice and said, "This place has made us all uneasy; so we are very glad to be leaving."

"As are we." Then turning to Caspar and Melchior, "I don't believe we should stop just now, let's get out of this city. Then we can change garments, consult our charts and the Royal Star."

All were in agreement; none of the magi looked behind or acted as though they were anything but happy to be continuing on their pilgrimage. Their security had been tightened during the time they were in Herod's throne room and each man was surrounded by personal guards as they finally got out of the palace and were swiftly on their way.

Back at the caravan that was waiting outside of the city walls; the magi were handed out of their fine clothing and jewels by their servants and fitted for travel. It was already evening and would soon be getting dark.

Meanwhile, the star seemed to be almost dancing. It blazed golden light in the night sky and its great arms beckoned them.

The caravan was happy to be moving and getting away from Herod's palace in Jerusalem.

Caspar and Melchior were shoulder to shoulder studying their maps; then with a shout, Melchior turned, saying "I have it! Look! We must be on our way to Bethlehem because His star is shining right above the city. Imagine! Bethlehem, the little town that is spoken of by the prophets of old. We will find our Lord will soon be born in the one of the least of the towns in Judea!"

Caspar wasn't sure, "But where? I know the Star beckons, but there is not one royal family in Bethlehem! There are no mighty palaces or fortresses! There is Herod's outlandish new palace, the Herodium, on the hillside overlooking Bethlehem, but we know He is not there."

Balthazar asked, "What does this mean? There is not one royal residence nearby. Where else would a great King be born?

"Maybe the answer is that they are in hiding?"

"No, Herod would know about any person of interest in his lands."

"What have we missed? Can it be true that after all we have seen and heard, we will not find the Royal Infant?" Caspar asked.

Melchior replied, "No! The angels have foretold His coming and the Royal Star is here, guiding us."

"We are not wrong," Balthazar added. "Maybe the answer is to look, and then look again at all the things we know."

Exasperated, Melchior started again, "Again, the Royal Infant, Son of the Most High, seems destined to be born in the tiniest of towns, a town that is poor without a royal household present. We have been told he will be found in a stable and we don't know the answer to that riddle at all. So, just where does one look for the Son of the Almighty? Shouldn't it be in a glorious palace, filled with royalty and with every advantage?"

They continued to follow the Royal Star as they pondered these questions.

It was still early night when Madai quickly approached Balthazar, "Majesty, we are coming across shepherds traveling into Bethlehem. It's very strange."

All three magi looked up, "What do you mean?"

"Sire, shepherds stay in the fields to guard their sheep; they don't just pick up and go into town. And they are many shepherds streaming into town, mostly one or two at a time; and there are a few small groups. They are all saying the same thing: they saw thousands of angels bringing tidings of a newborn king."

"Newborn? Please ask one of the shepherds to come here."

"Melchior, Caspar! Did you hear that? He has been born! The shepherds have seen angels declaring his birth and they have news about the Newborn and where he is! They are following the star into Bethlehem!"

One of the soldiers returned, "Your majesties, here is one of them."

Balthazar gazed into the dusk and saw a short, young man who was wearing the clothes of a shepherd and carrying a staff and a small lamb was tucked under his arm. He was obviously excited and a little afraid when he was brought before the magi.

He awkwardly bowed and excitedly started before he was asked, "Your majesties, have you heard? Have you seen? Angels, the sky was filled with angels and they were singing praises to God Almighty!

We all saw them!" he exclaimed and happily looked at each of them.

The magi all leaned forward and Balthazar said, "Please, tell us everything."

The shepherd continued, "I am one of the shepherds of the sheepfold and we are in the fields just out of town. It is late so everyone was sleeping but we never leave the sheep so we were in our robes and had a small fire. There are maybe three or four groups that have made campfires spread across the field while we watch at night.

However, I was awake out in the field because of this little one" and he glanced down at the tiny lamb sound asleep tucked close under his arm. "This one seems to wander away often so I had gone to find him and bring him back.

I had almost gotten back to the camp at the top of the hill when the sky started to glow! I thought that the big star was growing or something like that and when I looked up, I saw gold! Yes, the sky had turned golden because of an angel that was right there in the sky!

"He was singing praises. He said the son of the Almighty God has been born. Immanuel has been born in Bethlehem and is lying in a manager in a stable!"

The magi were growing more and more astonished. A real stable, not a royal palace and a manger that held cattle feed. They couldn't take their eyes off of the shepherd as he continued to tell them of the heavenly visit.

He continued, "But, majesties, then there were more angels and there were so many that they filled the sky! I swear! And they said to leave our fields and go worship Him!

We believe, so we have left our fields and are coming to worship Him!"

The magi had listened without talking, Balthazar then quickly thanked the shepherd so he could continue into town. The shepherd stepped back to his friends who had watched in wonder as their friend talked to magi! Then they all hastened on their way, singing and praising God for the gift of the Newborn King.

Caspar came up along Balthazar's side and looked at the other two, "A stable? What do you make of this? Is this our King? The King of kings and Lord of lords?"

Melchior said in wonder, "The Son of the Almighty who has come to establish His kingdom has not been born into wealthy nobility in a mighty palace or into a ruling earthly family but has arrived in this tiny town, heralded by a Royal Star and heavenly hosts singing Hallelujah!

And look! It must be true because the Royal Star has stopped and we are at our journey's end! It's even brighter now and its pure light is showing the way to the Newborn King! Come, we follow!"

Week 41

Bethlehem

"But you, Bethlehem Ephrathah, Though you are little among the thousands of Judah, Yet out of you shall come forth to Me The One to be Ruler in Israel, Whose goings forth are from of old, From everlasting."

The magi continued to ride across the fields that finally turned into dirt paths as they urged their camels to move quicker. They left most of the caravan behind in their haste as they followed the pure beam of light directly into Bethlehem. They would send word when they were close to finding the Royal Newborn, they would need to be at their best, then. They didn't stop or slow down, but hurried ahead and their personal attendants and security were the only ones that accompanied them.

They were still pondering what the shepherd had said, what the prophecies foretold and the fact that the Royal Star that was leading them into one of the smallest, unimportant towns in Judea to greet the Newborn Infant, Son of the Most High, who may be lying in an actual manger.

They still were unsure, how could He not be from a royal family with wealth and power? The prophecies clearly foretold Him; so they had always believed He would be a powerful warrior king that would lead the Jews in mighty battles to defeat the Romans who ruled them now and then create His kingdom. How else do you destroy powerful enemies and how else do you win control and establish a kingdom?

But the angels said nothing about this; instead they said He was in a stable lying in a manger? This still seemed to make no sense and why couldn't they make any sense about the manger?

Finally Balthazar simply said, "I do not understand. I have come to know this Lord of lords, I believe; but I don't understand His lowly birth. No wealth. No privilege. No power. The only Son of the Almighty in a stable! How can He be served if He is born as a servant?"

"It is becoming clearer to me. The Royal Infant is not here to be served, He has come to serve. He has entered this world to establish His kingdom, but not through bloodshed, He has entered this world to show us the way to His Father, to save us all. His authority comes from above, God Almighty, His Father, and doesn't need the fleeting authority of this world", said Melchior.

As the magi were talking, they and their attendants entered Bethlehem. It seemed filled to overflowing with men and their entire families who were there to register for the taxes as ordered by Caesar. Thankfully, they were exhausted from their long journeys and would soon be sound asleep at inns. There were no royal announcements posted, there were no grand trumpets announcing the birth of a Son.

Balthazar signaled to Japheth, "Send riders through the town to ask if there is any news. Don't tell them who we are looking for. Just ask for news and please hurry."

He dipped his head, "At once, sire!"

It was dark and quiet, shepherds continued to walk quickly into the town and follow the beam of light that shone directly down from the star. The Herodium, the giant palace built by King Herod, crouched on the hill above the town, its shadow even darker than the night.

The magi slowly followed any of the shepherds that they saw walking purposefully. They were starting to understand that their journey had finally brought them to the Newborn King's birthplace and He was very close by.

They were humbled and jubilant; in fact, they felt like shouting and singing! The shepherds continued to come into the village out of the fields and some had sheep on their shoulders and hurried along with friends. They could overhear parts of their conversations clearly and they were exclaiming about the thousands of angels in the skies above the fields.

Caspar was becoming more excited and finally blurted out, "I can't wait! Let's join the others and go see the Newborn!"

Balthazar nodded, "After all of this time, we will finally see His face!"

Melchior put out a hand, "We can't go like this! Unlike the good people we see here, we know exactly who this Newborn is so we have more of a responsibility. We can't greet Him unless we are giving Him our hearts and our very best, our all."

They looked at each other and agreed, "Let all who see us know that we are magi and we have come to worship Him with the very best that we have and that we hold nothing back. We may look different than the shepherds and other visitors but we are really all alike in our love for the King."

Balthazar called Illya, "I need to be presentable to the Son of God and I mean right now."

Illya started and for once was quiet, "Yes, majesty."

The other magi summoned their own servants. They quickly obtained their trunks from the caravans and were soon surrounded by multiple body servants to be dressed for the most important event in their lives.

"And you have 15 minutes to accomplish this, Illya."

In no more than 15 minutes the magi were gathering for the final part of their journey, the ride down the streets of Bethlehem, following the glowing beam from the Royal Star.

They were each so different than when they started on their journey. They had been blessed by their faith and the power of mercy and now they would be given something even greater—this gift of their heart's desire.

~~~~~~~~~~~~~~~~~~~~

They were handed up onto their camels and at once they arranged themselves so they would be able to greet the Newborn and honor Him with their gifts in perfect order; befitting the Son of the Most High God.

The little town was quiet, most people were now asleep and the torches that lit several of the inns were getting low as straggling travelers finished late meals. It was amazing; the giant royal star was straight above them and soft amber light shown down clearly illuminating the path. Outside of the light, all was in darkness and those in the dark seemed not to listen to the shepherds' joyful songs and shouts of joy.

The magi rode together closely, saying nothing but watching everything.

As they turned down a dark lane, Caspar leaned toward the others, pointed and softly spoke, "Look, there is something there. I see something next to that small inn directly in front of us on the side of the hill. It is so dark that it's hard to see."

Shepherds had stopped at the side of the dusty path and were on their knees gazing ahead into a stable. There was no sound and the quiet had become breathtaking, as if the world itself could not believe the gift.

The royal star stopped moving and majestically changed its form. A soft clean brilliance now spilled out from heaven onto the earth and straight down into a tiny stable, illuminating the small humble group on their knees in front of a young couple with a newborn child.

Week 42

Immanuel

✍

"For God so loved the world that He gave His
only begotten Son. That whoever believes in
Him will not perish but have everlasting life."

The three magi were still. They could clearly see the shape
of the baby that was the Divine Newborn King. They
recognized Him as the Divine King of kings, and He was lying
in a manger in a stable! A sturdy young man, who looked as
though he would be much more comfortable out in a workshop
and tending to his craft, was standing at the side and slightly
behind the baby. A young Jewish girl who had to be His mother
picked Him up and held Him close to her heart. They looked
like simple hardworking people who were surprised by the
shepherds and others who had gathered to them.

The Newborn's mother was the first to see the three kings
as they began to slowly appear out of the darkness and come
into the light. They looked very regal and their clothing and
jewels showed them to be revered magi, royal monarchs. She
watched them carefully as she seemed to commit everything
to memory.

As they approached, Balthazar saw the small hand of the
Holy One that seemed to wave in delight. His heart saw the
light that was sent by God to illuminate the dark world, to show

that kindness and mercy is what He requires from servant and king alike.

Caspar heard the sigh of the Royal Newborn. His heart heard the voice of Almighty God, telling the world of His love for us all,

Melchior's heart recognized Him and he knew this baby was the truth and healing that he had sought all of his life. His whole spirit sang! He was seeing the Promised One, Immanuel.

The magi's attendants handed them down from their camels. Balthazar was curious and looked at the others that were greeting the Newborn. There were other travelers; prosperous and not so prosperous, and the shepherds who obviously had been visited by angels. Their faces shone with heavenly light and it was apparent that they also recognized the little baby as Lord. Several simply kneeled and gazed in silence at Him, occasionally one or two would quietly leave and then could be seen dashing to others, telling them the story that the angels proclaimed.

But at the manger, no one spoke and in the silence they could hear the baby sigh.

Balthazar knew the time had come so he held his hands out to Illya to retrieve his gift for the Divine Newborn King and he received the golden chest, his offering to God. He then turned to the stable and knelt.

The shepherds and villagers were looking into the stable at the manger. Balthazar waited quietly until he felt he could raise his head and look questioningly at the Newborn's father. The young man was overwhelmed; he couldn't stop looking at the Newborn, which was apparently his son; his wife, and then the magi that were arrayed some yards in front of them in their most regal clothes.

Balthazar saw a small nod from the mother and so he moved forward to his King. He felt Caspar and Melchior move somewhere behind him.

Caspar couldn't take his eyes from the Royal Infant. His wide-eyed attendant wordlessly placed the priceless casket of frankincense in his hands. The very air around the stable seemed to shimmer and dance with joy at the birth. Caspar's soul sang; his heart heard the message of love that this new-born brought with Him from His Father. He believed the truth of the promises that the Father sent to all that followed His beloved Son, that there was an eternal home for all where there was no more sickness, sorrow or death.

Melchior grasped the bejeweled container of myrrh that he had brought for his offering to the King of kings. At once he felt an overwhelming joy and he raised his face to see the sky filled with angels, row after row of them singing with joy. They were celebrating the wonder of the King of kings born on earth. He felt the air move around him and angels were standing and moving all around him. There were so many that he couldn't count them all.

His mouth dropped open and then he heard a quiet voice in his heart, "Why are you surprised, Melchior? You have believed the true words of the prophets of the Most High and you have followed them straight to your King. Rejoice! He has been given for you and to the entire world to save you so none will ever walk in darkness again."

He had not understood why he had felt that this gift was exactly what he should bring, until now—myrrh was the perfect gift for the One who was the Perfect Sacrifice and High Priest to the world.

Meanwhile Balthazar approached the stable directly in front of the manger, and again, he saw that picture in his mind. He was on his knee, giving his kingdom and royal authority away but now he knew the gesture wasn't one of defeat and humiliation. In reality he had been offered the greater ever-lasting kingdom of truth and peace by Almighty God and by following the Son, he would live and reign with him.

The picture left his mind and again he saw the manger. In great ceremony Balthazar knelt onto one knee and then brought the other knee down and lowered his forehead to the ground and paused. He raised himself to his knee again to look directly into the lovely eyes of the mother, saying "I humbly wish to greet the Newborn King of kings and Lord of Lords and then drew his gaze to the Newborn who was patiently looking back at him. I present myself, my heart and every part of my being in service to You. I offer this small token of esteem to My Lord – gold, the gift for a king."

Balthazar stretched forward and placed the priceless golden vase at the foot of the manger. He again knelt low, bringing his forehead to the ground and paused.

When he raised himself he looked fully into the face of the Son of God. He was perfect and when he looked back at Balthazar, his soul was cleansed. His spirit soared and He knew he had been accepted by the Most High. He was changed, his entire life belonged to the One who would never leave him or forsake him. Because of His presence, Balthazar would never be the same and there would be no more devastating anxieties.

Caspar was on his knees behind Balthazar and as Balthazar backed slowly to the side, Caspar rose and came forward and then knelt low with his forehead to the ground.

He straightened saying, "I also humbly ask to greet the Newborn King of kings, offering myself, my heart and all I have to you, my Lord." Caspar had been speaking first to the parents of the infant, and then gazed at the child. "I wish to present this humble token of my love for You–frankincense, the gift for a priest."

The baby wasn't sleeping like other newborns would have been; He seemed to have a lively interest in His world to which he had recently arrived. He watched as Caspar solemnly turned to Him and their eyes met. Caspar immediately felt the outflow of love and grace and clearly heard the truth of the Almighty God in the coos of the baby.

He told Caspar that he was loved and that those who followed Him were to love God above all things, and to love one another. Caspar remained still as his heart continued to hear words of encouragement and peace. After a moment he placed his gift next to Balthazar's at the manger and then bowing low again, moved back and to the side.

Melchior came last, he had been kneeling while Balthazar and Caspar presented their offerings and he had watched everything. He rose and came forward, bowed himself to the ground, and then slowly straightened saying, "Allow me to humbly offer my greetings and worship to the Newborn Son of God. I gladly offer myself, my heart and everything that is within me to you, my Lord."

He came forward slightly, "I have only this small token of my heart with which to honor you—myrrh, the gift for a healer and for the perfect sacrifice." He placed the diamond-encrusted bottle next to the gifts presented by the other magi.

Melchior was overcome with emotion and could not continue to speak as he looked at the Newborn. The baby turned and stretched out toward him and Melchior could not help but smile.

Melchior knew he had been created for this moment and he would spend the rest of his life telling others of the truth of the Son of God, who had come to this world to establish his kingdom forever by saving those who would follow him. Melchior had already received what his heart yearned for: truth, peace, and goodness.

He knelt again and all three magi stayed in place for a moment more, looking at their Savior and King, then it was time to go. They slowly backed away, straightened, bowed again and then left. As they approached their attendants, they looked up and could still see the star above, shining down softly on Immanuel, the eternal Lord of Lords and King of Kings who was Light to the dark earth. They could hear the shouts of the shepherds as they ran to tell others of the angels and their proclamations.

They were soon on their camels, weaving their way through the streets of tiny Bethlehem to return to their caravan. They were changed out of their gowns, and their personal jewels and priceless gowns were all returned to chests for safekeeping. It was time to go home.

Elated Caspar shouted over his shoulder to his friends, "This is a marvelous end to our adventure!"

"End? No, the beginning!" chuckled Balthazar.

Melchior couldn't stop from laughing in joy because of the hope and salvation that he knew had come down to earth that night for everyone.

They could feel the new life in them, the everlasting life that rested in them, in the presence and in their belief in the one called the Lord of lords, Jesus the Christ. They and all believers had been given the greatest gift of all – Immanuel, God With Us.

The End

Or in the words of Balthazar, The Beginning

About the Author

Rhonda Quillin, by day, is the editor for the Department of Tactics at the US Army Command and General Staff College. Otherwise, she writes fiction. Watch for her next book, *We Were Called Out.*

She lives with her husband, Charlie, among vintage dogs, cats, and a fantastic 1968 Camaro.

CPSIA information can be obtained at www.ICGtesting.com
Printed in the USA
LVOW06s1250260714

396070LV00002B/152/P